P9-AFI-128

A Streetcar Named Desire
The Moth and the Lantern

Twayne's Masterwork Studies

Robert Lecker, General Editor

A Streetcar Named Desire
The Moth and the Lantern

Thomas P. Adler

Twayne Publishers • Boston
A Division of G.K. Hall & Co.

A Streetcar Named Desire: The Moth and the Lantern
Thomas P. Adler

Twayne's Masterwork Studies No. 47
Copyright 1990 by G.K. Hall & Co.
All rights reserved.
Published by Twayne Publishers
A Division of G.K. Hall & Co.
70 Lincoln Street
Boston, Massachusetts 02111

Copyediting supervised by Barbara Sutton
Book production by Gabrielle B. McDonald

Typeset in 10 point Sabon, display type set in Meridien
by Huron Valley Graphics, Inc. of Ann Arbor, Michigan

Printed on permanent/durable acid-free paper
and bound in the United States of America

Library of Congress Cataloging-in-Publication Data

Adler, Thomas P.
    A streetcar named Desire : the moth and the lantern / Thomas P.
Adler.
        p.   cm.—(Twayne's masterwork studies ; no. 47)
    Includes bibliographical references.
    1. Williams, Tennessee, 1911–1983. Streetcar named desire.
I. Title.   II. Series.
PS3545.I5365S8228   1990
812'.54—dc20   89-38927
                                                                    CIP

0.8057.7994.9 (alk. paper) 10 9 8 7 6 5 4 3 2 1
0.8057.8043.2 (pbk. : alk. paper) 10 9 8 7 6 5 4 3 2 1

Contents

Note on the References and Acknowledgments

Quotations from *A Streetcar Named Desire* throughout this monograph refer to the New Directions paperback edition, first published in 1980.

As I finish this manuscript, the professoriate continues to be assailed by charges of overspecialization and politicization. The jeremiad has gone out accusing us of having failed to make the arts and the humanities come alive, not only for our students but for the American people as well. A book like this—and the series in which it appears— can perhaps dispel some of those accusations, since the intended audience is the general reader in the classroom, library or living room, who confronts one of the major texts in world literature, hoping to appreciate its wonders.

What follows is, nevertheless, grounded in the available scholarship: my method has involved repeatedly renewing my acquaintance with Williams's text, while at the same time researching widely what others have written about *A Streetcar Named Desire*—but then "forgetting," or at least holding in abeyance, most of that material. My intention has been to arrive at a fresh—dare I hope original—analysis and interpretation of the play, largely unencumbered by scholarly apparatus. Undoubtedly, what others have said has lodged in my memory, or jogged my mind to move in directions that it otherwise might not have, and for that I remain grateful. I especially want to acknowledge the earlier work that Jordan Miller and Mary Ann Corrigan and Bert Cardullo have done on *Streetcar* to open up the text in new and exciting ways.

My specific debts, and thus my particular appreciation, go to the librarians in the Interlibrary Loan Office at Purdue University; to the staff of the Billy Rose Theatre Collection of the Library for the Performing Arts at Lincoln Center; to Wendy Howard, not only for typing the next-to-final draft of this manuscript but for leading me tirelessly through the intricacies of a new word processing system; and to Peggy Fox of New Directions for helping me secure permission to quote from Williams's plays and essays.

The striking photograph of the dramatist reproduced here comes from my own collection, Williams's agent having supplied it prior to the playwright's visit to Purdue in 1972. My best efforts to track down the name of the photographer have gone unrewarded: neither Lyle Leverich, who is preparing the authorized biography of the playwright; nor Robert Lantz, the literary agent for the estate of Tennessee Williams; nor the Lady Maria St. Just, a trustee of the estate who responded through Mr. Lantz; nor anyone at New Directions, seems to have knowledge of the photo, which I assume was taken in the early 1970s. I am, however, grateful for the time they took to respond to my inquiries, and will, of course, appropriately acknowledge the photographer in any future editions should he or she come forward. The other two illustrations appear through the kind permission of the Harry Ransom Humanities Research Center Library at the University of Texas at Austin, and I sincerely appreciate Cathy Henderson's help in searching the collection there.

As always, special thanks to my wife and sons who have learned to live with me patiently through the writing of each book. Finally, I would like to dedicate this monograph to the memory of my first teacher of modern drama at Boston College, the late Edward Nehls, and to all the many students with whom I have talked about American theater over the past twenty-five years. May this little book speak to its readers as if we were in a room together, so that they might come to understand and value *Streetcar* more with each exposure to it, as I have.

•   •   •

Note on the References and Acknowledgments

Excerpts from Tennessee Williams's *A Streetcar Named Desire*, copyright 1947 by Tennessee Williams; *The Glass Menagerie*, copyright 1945 by Tennessee Williams and Edwina Williams; *The Night of the Iguana* from *The Theater of Tennessee Williams*, vol. 4; and *Where I Live*, © 1978 by Tennessee Williams are reprinted by permission of New Directions Publishing Corporation.

Tennessee Williams in the early Seventies.
Provided to the author by Tennessee Williams; photographer unknown.

Chronology: Tennessee Williams's Life and Works

1911	Thomas Lanier Williams born 26 March to Cornelius Coffin and Edwina Dakin Williams, in Columbus, Mississippi. Sister Rose Isabel born in 1909. During the extended periods the father is on the road as a shoe company salesman, the family resides with the maternal grandparents in the parsonage of St. Paul's Episcopal Church, where the Reverand Walter Dakin is rector.
1913–1918	Lives in various locations in Tennessee and Mississippi. Becomes withdrawn after a long bout with diphtheria and a kidney infection.
1918	When father becomes branch manager for shoe company, the family moves in July to St. Louis, Missouri where they live in a succession of apartments and later houses. Father taunts Tom for his difference by nicknaming him "Miss Nancy."
1919	Brother Walter Dakin born.
1924–1926	Taking refuge from his pathological shyness in creativity, writes a ghost story for the junior high school newspaper, and later poems for the high school paper; finds his first girlfriend in Hazel Kramer.
1927	Becomes a published writer with the essay, "Can a Good Wife Be a Good Sport?" in *Smart Set*, for which he receives third prize. Also wins a prize for a movie review of *Stella Dallas*.
1928	First short story, "The Vengeance of Nitocris," printed in *Weird Tales* in July. Sees his first Broadway play, the Kern/Hammerstein/Ferber musical *Show Boat*, and then tours Europe with his maternal grandfather.
1929	Enters the University of Missouri in September, where he joins a fraternity. Becomes the first freshman ever to receive honorable mention in contest (for a play, *Beauty Is the Word*.) Befriends fellow poet Esmeralda Mayer.

1931   Sees Alla Nazimova perform in Henrik Ibsen's *Ghosts*. Father withdraws him from the university for flunking ROTC. Begins work as a clerk in the warehouse at the International Shoe Co. and pursues his writing at home during the night. Votes for Socialist Norman Thomas for president.

1934   Story "Stella for Star" wins first place in amateur contest.

1935   Suffers a breakdown and goes to recuperate for a year at maternal grandparents' home in Memphis; during this period becomes enthralled with Anton Chekhov's dramas. First production of his play *Cairo! Shanghai! Bombay!* by Memphis Garden Players on 12 July.

1936   Enrolls in Washington University, St. Louis, where he reads Hart Crane, publishes poetry in college magazine, and wins top prize in a poetry contest. The Mummers produce several plays, including *Candles in the Sun* and, the next year, *The Fugitive Kind*, which garner Williams his first notable reviews as a promising dramatist. His story "27 Wagons Full of Cotton," later adapted into two plays and a film, appears.

1937   Transfers to the University of Iowa where he enrolls in E. P. Conkle's and E. C. Mabie's famous playwriting class. His sister, Rose, undergoes prefrontal lobotomy.

1938   In August receives degree in English from Iowa.

1939   Lives briefly in a number of locations in the Midwest, South, and West, including New Orleans—which becomes his favorite city and where he has his first homosexual experience—and Taos, New Mexico, where he meets D. H. Lawrence's widow. First uses the name "Tennessee" as the author of "The Field of Blue Children," published in *Story* magazine. Greatly encouraged by a $100 prize from the Theatre Guild for a collection of one-act plays called *American Blues*, as well as a $1,000 grant from the Rockefeller Foundation, he hires Audrey Wood as his literary agent.

1940   Takes John Gassner's seminar in advanced playwriting at the New School for Social Research in New York City, which stages *The Long Goodbye*, his first play to be seen there; they will later (in 1942) present *This Property is Condemned* on a bill with works by J. M. Synge, August Strindberg, and Molière. Lives briefly in Mexico and in Provincetown on Cape Cod, where he has his first sustained homosexual relationship. *Battle of Angels*, directed by Margaret Webster and starring Miriam Hopkins, opens on 30 December in Boston before an outraged audience and quickly closes; is revised as *Orpheus Descending* in 1957.

1941–1942   Lives in a variety of locations, including Key West, Florida, and New Orleans (both places where he will later own homes), and works at a variety of jobs.

1943   Leaves being an usher at the Strand Theatre on Broadway to go to California, when MGM hires him to write a filmscript for Lana Turner. Works also on a screenplay entitled *The Gentleman Caller*, which will be revised into his first big theatrical success. *You Touched Me!*, dramatized with Donald Windham from a Lawrence short story and directed by Guthrie McClintic, is produced in Cleveland and Pasadena (and in 1945 in New York).

1944   *The Glass Menagerie*, starring the legendary Laurette Taylor in her final role and directed by Eddie Dowling, premieres 26 December in Chicago and is kept alive by the critics.

1945   *The Glass Menagerie* opens on Broadway 31 March and wins the New York Drama Critics' Circle, Donaldson, and Sidney Howard Memorial awards; Williams signs over half of all royalties to his mother. Undergoes last of four unsuccessful operations for cataract on his left eye.

1946   *27 Wagons Full of Cotton and Other One-Act Plays* published. Begins a longtime friendship with the southern novelist Carson McCullers.

1947   *A Streetcar Named Desire*, produced by Irene Mayer Selznick, directed by Elia Kazan, and designed by Jo Mielziner, starring Jessica Tandy, Marlon Brando, Karl Malden, and Kim Stanley, opens on Broadway 3 December and wins the Pulitzer Prize for drama, as well as the New York Critics' Circle and Donaldson awards, making it the first work ever to take all three. Continues for 885 performances, the longest Broadway run of any Williams play.

1948   The playwright's parents separate. *Summer and Smoke*, directed by Margo Jones, is produced on Broadway 6 October; revived off-Broadway in 1952 with Geraldine Page under the direction of José Quintero and later revised as *The Eccentricities of a Nightingale* in 1976. A first collection of fiction, *One Arm and Other Stories*, published. Visits Paris and Rome, where he meets Gore Vidal and Truman Capote. Begins a fourteen-year intimacy with Frank Merlo.

1950   A novel, *The Roman Spring of Mrs. Stone*, brought out. Film version of *The Glass Menagerie* released.

1951   *The Rose Tattoo*, produced by Cheryl Crawford and directed by Daniel Mann, premieres 27 February and receives Tony Award for best play. A short play about D. H. Lawrence, *I Rise in Flame, Cried the Phoenix*, appears. Film version of *Streetcar*, with Vivien Leigh as Blanche, released.

1952   Elected to the National Institute of Arts and Letters.

1953   *Camino Real*, directed by Kazan, produced unsuccessfully 19 March.

1954   Publishes *Hard Candy: A Book of Stories*.

1955   *Cat on a Hot Tin Roof*, starring Barbara Bel Geddes, Ben Gazzara, and Burl Ives under the direction of Kazan (who urged the writing of a new third act), opens on Broadway 24 March and wins the New York Critics' Circle Award and Pulitzer Prize. Williams's grandfather dies at age ninety-seven. Film version of *Rose Tattoo*, featuring Anna Magnani in a famous performance, is released.

1956   Controversial film *Baby Doll*, directed by Kazan and starring Carroll Baker, premieres amidst a censorship furor fueled by New York's Cardinal Spellman; is revised for stage as *Tiger Tail*, 1978. A first collection of poems, *In the Winter of Cities*, published. Williams's dependence on artificial stimulants in order to write begins.

1957   *Orpheus Descending*, directed by Harold Clurman, opens on Broadway 21 March. Williams's father dies. The playwright begins a year of psychoanalysis with Dr. Lawrence Kubie.

1958   *Garden District* (composed of *Something Unspoken* and *Suddenly Last Summer*) produced off-Broadway with Anne Meacham under the direction of Herbert Machiz, 7 January. Film version of *Cat*, starring Elizabeth Taylor and Paul Newman, released.

1959   *Sweet Bird of Youth*, starring Page and Newman and with Kazan again directing, opens 10 March. Williams goes to Havanna to meet Fidel Castro, who had performed on stage and is interested in movies. Screen version of *Suddenly Last Summer*, directed by Joseph Mankiewicz and starring Taylor, Katharine Hepburn, and Montgomery Clift, released.

1960   Williams's only comedy, *Period of Adjustment*, premieres 10 November, directed by George Roy Hill. Film *The Fugitive Kind*, starring Brando and Magnani under the direction of Sidney Lumet, opens.

1961   *The Night of the Iguana*, Williams's last Broadway success, premieres 28 December with Bette Davis, Margaret Leighton,

	and Alan Webb under Frank Corsaro's direction; wins for playwright his fourth New York Critics' Circle Award.
1962	Williams appears on the cover of *Time;* is elected to member-ship in the American Academy of Arts and Letters. Original version of *The Milk Train Doesn't Stop Here Anymore* pro-duced at the festival in Spoleto, Italy; revised versions appear in New York on Broadway in 1963 and 1964, with Tallulah Bankhead. Film version of *Sweet Bird,* directed by Richard Brooks, and *Period of Adjustment,* directed by Hill, released.
1963	Intimate friend, Frank Merlo, whom Williams first began liv-ing with in 1947, dies of cancer. Williams enters period of depression he refers to as his "Stoned Age."
1964	Film version of *The Night of the Iguana,* with Richard Bur-ton, Ava Gardner, and Sue Lyon, directed by John Houston, released.
1965	Brandeis University bestows Creative Arts Award.
1966	*Slapstick Tragedy* (comprised of *The Mutilated* and *The Gnä-diges Fräulein* and featuring Margret Leighton, Kate Reid, and Zoë Caldwell) opens on Broadway 22 February. Williams be-coming increasingly dependent on drugs. Film of *This Prop-erty is Condemned,* directed by Sidney Pollack, released.
1967	*The Knightly Quest: A Novella and Four Short Stories* ap-pears. Initial version of *The Two-Character Play* premieres at Hampstead Theatre Club in London; revised as *Out Cry* for productions in Chicago (1971) and New York (3 March 1973, directed by Peter Glenville) and revised further under original title for performance in San Francisco in 1976.
1968	*The Seven Descents of Myrtle,* under the direction of José Quintero, opens 27 March; produced in revised version as *Kingdom of Earth* at Princeton, New Jersey, in 1975. *Boom!,* the film version of *Milk Train* with Taylor and Burton under the direction of Joseph Losey, opens.
1969	Is baptized as a Roman Catholic on 6 January in Key West. Awarded an honorary doctor of humane letters from the Uni-versity of Missouri–Columbia and the Gold Medal for Drama from the National Institute of Arts and Letters. *In the Bar of a Tokyo Hotel* produced off-Broadway 11 May. Travels to Ja-pan. Enters Barnes Hospital, St. Louis, for psychiatric care, September–December.
1970	*Dragon Country: A Book of Plays* appears.
1971	Audrey Wood, who served as Williams's literary agent for thirty-two years, is replaced by Bill Barnes. New Directions

begins bringing out *The Theatre of Tennessee Williams* (in seven volumes, through 1981). Williams speaks openly against the war at an anti-Vietnam War rally.

1972   *Small Craft Warnings* opens under the direction of Robert Altman for a successful run off-Broadway on 2 April, with Williams taking over the role of Doc for a brief period.

1973   Awarded the first Centennial Medal of the Cathedral of St. John the Divine. Notorious *Playboy* interview appears in April.

1974   *Eight Mortal Ladies Possessed,* a fourth collection of short fiction, published.

1975   The National Arts Club awards Williams its Medal of Honor for Literature. A second novel, *Moise and the World of Reason,* and his autobiographical *Memoirs,* which deals openly with his homosexuality, are both published. *The Red Devil Battery Sign,* with Anthony Quinn and Claire Bloom, plays briefly in Boston; revised versions are later produced in Vienna (1976) and London (1977).

1976   *The Demolition Downtown* produced in London. *This is (An Entertainment)* mounted in San Francisco. PBS television documentary "Tennessee Williams's South" is broadcast. *Letters to Donald Windham 1940–1965* published.

1977   *Vieux Carré* opens 11 May, starring Sylvia Sidney. A second volume of poems, *Androgyne, Mon Amour,* appears.

1978   *Crève Coeur* (revised as *A Lovely Sunday for Crève Coeur* the following year) plays at the Spoleto Festival USA in Charleston, South Carolina. A collection of prose, *Where I Live: Selected Essays,* appears. Mitch Douglas becomes Williams's third literary agent.

1979   *Kirche, Kutchen, und Kinder* is produced beginning September.

1980   Williams's mother dies. The dramatist receives the Medal of Freedom from President Carter. *Will Mr. Merriwether Return from Memphis?* inaugurates the Tennessee Williams Performing Arts Center in Key West on 24 January. *Clothes for a Summer Hotel,* Williams final full-length play to be staged in New York, opens 26 March, the playwright's sixty-ninth birthday. Serves a brief tenure as Distinguished Writer-in-Residence at the University of British Columbia.

1981   *A House Not Meant to Stand* premieres at the Goodman Theatre in Chicago, the city that witnessed Williams's birth as a successful dramatist; and *Something Cloudy, Something Clear,* his last play to be produced in New York during his lifetime, opens 24 August. He (along with Harold Pinter, who called Williams "the greatest American playwright") wins the prestigious Common Wealth Award, which carries an $11,000 prize.

1982   Harvard University confers honorary doctorate.

1983   Dies 24 or 25 February at the Hotel Élysée in New York, apparently from choking on a cap from a medicine bottle. Is buried in St. Louis, against his expressed wish to be buried at sea, like Hart Crane.

1984   Publication of *Stopped Rocking and Other Screenplays*.

1985   New Directions brings out *Tennessee Williams: The Collected Stories*, with an introduction by Gore Vidal.

1986   *Ten by Tennessee*, two evenings of one-act plays, produced in May in New York. Selected interviews, *Conversations with Tennessee Williams*, appears.

1

Historical Context

Although any overview of a historical period will tend to simplify matters, even a broad perspective can help us situate and thus better understand such national cultural treasures as *A Streetcar Named Desire*. In his introduction to *The 1940's: Profile of a Nation in Crisis*, Chester Eisinger delineates the mood of the decade as "one of fear, terror, uncertainty, and violence, mingled with sad satisfactions and a relief at victory." It was the decade of the war and its aftermath: the former characterized by "fear of death," the latter by "fear of the bomb and of the government." The bomb could, of course, end civilization itself; the government potentially could foster a cold war paranoia and xenophobia in the face of a supposed Communist threat—and a well-intentioned if overzealous segment of it in fact did. The effect upon the citizenry, Eisinger argues, was a regimentation and depersonalization not only within the military during the war but within business and labor in the postwar years. Corporations demanded conformity from their "organization" men, and even the unions fostered an atmosphere of "impersonality" that was "inhospitable to . . . the idiosyncratic self."[1]

Eisinger claims this increasing dehumanization finds reflection in the literature and the art of the period, with their themes of "the quest for identity" and "the alienation of man from the self and from society," as well as a concomitant shift away "from social consciousness to aestheticism." The shifts in social class and status resulting from the New Deal of the thirties and the wartime economy of the forties caused many people to feel a sense of dislocation. Their resulting search for belonging and connection led them to look to the past to discover some "stability."

For some playwrights who achieved prominence during the forties, such as Arthur Miller, the movement toward aesthetic issues and away from the social concerns and commitment that had dominated the plays of Elmer Rice in the twenties and Clifford Odets in the thirties—and that would later energize the black writers of the fifties and sixties—is not, however, nearly so dramatic as Eisinger would suggest. Though he is formally experimental and adventuresome, in *Death of a Salesman* (1949) social consciousness is uppermost, as Miller castigates the way in which the promises of the American Dream have been perverted into a success-at-any-price syndrome. In his first notable Broadway achievement, *All My Sons* (1947), Miller wrote about America at war: blinded by the profit motive, an airplane-parts manufacturer denies his social responsibility and inadvertently causes the death of his own son. In *The Crucible* from the early fifties, Miller dramatizes the paranoia and fear created through the atmosphere of suspicion and guilt-by-association that Eisinger sees as characteristic of the postwar years. Here the Salem witch hunts provide an analogy for the workings of the House Un-American Activities Committee, which came to be known in the popular mind as the Army/McCarthy hearings.

Tennessee Williams, the other distinguished dramatist of the postwar period, is—unlike Miller—not *primarily* a social playwright. Yet his works do still reflect a number of the themes that Eisinger finds in the forties, including concern with isolation, alienation, and identity. Williams evidences, however, a much more pronounced shift toward a consideration of aesthetic issues than does his fellow playwright Miller. Within *The Glass Menagerie* (1945), structured as a guilt play in which the narrator/central character attempts to come to terms with having followed the imperative of individuating himself as a man and developing himself as an artist over his responsibility to care for his sister and mother, Williams positions a number of comments about a world on the verge of conflagration; but, as his narrator notes, Americans by and large are too concerned with their country's own social disturbances—economic depression and labor unrest—to pay much attention to a civil war in Spain. As the time of *Menagerie* proceeds to Chamberlain and the Munich Pact, and the rest of the "world was waiting for bombardments," Americans were still escaping reality through dance halls and bars, movies and sex. Yet by the end of the play, history has caught up with them: now, in the narrator's words, "the world is lit by lightning!" If Tom Wingfield, Williams's authorial figure, faces questions of conscience having to do with responsibility, so, too, does America, whose growth of consciousness from isolation to involvement is charted in the hazily presented social and political background of *Menagerie*.

A Streetcar Named Desire examines post–World War II America. The play, however, does not reflect the suspicion and guilt-by-association mentality that will come to dominate the early fifties, as *Cat on a Hot Tin Roof* (1955) with its unsubstantiated charges of homosexuality against Brick and its more generalized condemnation of mendacity can be seen as doing. Rather, *Streetcar* looks, however fleetingly, at the returning soldier/officer who must now be reintegrated into a work force (recently vacated by women whose temporary careers outside the home have been snapped out from under them). The veterans face jobs that are often just as unrewarding and impersonal as the military and a society not yet doing a great deal for those who had served. Their new lives appear closer to drudgery than an opportunity to reap the benefits of the American Dream they fought to preserve and protect.

Early in his stage directions for *Streetcar*, Williams singles out the somewhat easy, if atypical, camaraderie between blacks and whites that could be found in the French Quarter of New Orleans, and in so doing, implicitly recognizes the deeply entrenched racial segregation of the war years—particularly in the military. As the most prominent of

America's southern dramatists (Lillian Hellman, author of *The Little Foxes* and *Toys in the Attic,* and most recently Beth Henley, who wrote *Crimes of the Heart,* are two others), Williams might he expected to attend to racial questions more than he actually does in his full-length works. *Portrait of a Madonna* (1946), a short play considered a preliminary study for *Streetcar,* prominently features a black porter whose role is to modulate the response of the theater audience and to serve as its moral norm. *Madonna* tells the story of a sexually frustrated and neurotic spinster whose upbringing in a succession of southern rectories under the nay-saying and guilt-inducing "shadow" of the church and the cross has left her totally unprepared for life and prey to crazed illusions; the Los Angeles premiere starred Jessica Tandy, whose performance in the role won her the part of Blanche DuBois in *Streetcar.* Lucretia Collins, the virginal madonna of the title, who hallucinates that she is pregnant by a former beau, faces eviction from her flat and commitment to a sanatorium; the compassionate black Porter insists on treating her always as the "lady" she prides herself on being, while the cynical and crude Elevator Boy finds her a "disgusting" freak. If these two foil characters do, in fact, act as an onstage audience to Lucretia's creative illusions, then it appears Williams is working out in a sketchy way the theater metaphor that he will develop in *Streetcar:* Lucretia's bedroom of illusions is her stage where she can escape from a world of reality into a realm of magic; and her final madness becomes a saving grace that renders permanent the life created by the imagination.

The Lady of Larkspur Lotion, another one-act play dating from the same period, cries out even more explicitly and poignantly for a recognition of "God-given imagination" as a compensation "for the cruel deficiencies of reality." In it, the Writer pleads with Mrs. Wire, his landlady, that she exercise "compassion and understanding" and allow another of her tenants, Mrs. Hardwicke-Moore, the comfort that believing in illusion can bring. The Writer, who in the curtain line declares himself to be "Anton Pavlovitch Chekhov" (one of the central influences on Williams himself), pleads that his own "dreams and fictions and fancies" not be destroyed and labeled "a *lie*" by Mrs.

Wire, which is how Stanley Kowalski will label Blanche's fantasies and, later, even her truthful accusations against him in *Streetcar*.

The successes of *The Glass Menagerie* and *A Streetcar Named Desire* ushered in Williams's most fertile period as a dramatist. In rapid succession, New York audiences saw productions of *Summer and Smoke* (1948), *The Rose Tattoo* (1951), *Cat on a Hot Tin Roof* (1955), *Suddenly Last Summer* (1958), *Sweet Bird of Youth* (1959), and *The Night of the Iguana* (1961). A *Time* cover story (9 March 1962) declared Williams, "barring the aged Sean O'Casey, the greatest living playwright anywhere."[2] Although in the last twenty years of his life Williams would never again achieve commercial success and most often faced a drumming from the critics, he kept writing and revising incessantly. Works such as *In the Bar of a Tokyo Hotel* (1969), *Out Cry* (1971), and *Clothes for a Summer Hotel* (1980) became ever more personal as they focused more obsessively on the artist figure. At the end of his life in the early eighties, though the proviso "along with Samuel Beckett and Harold Pinter" would need to be added, the *Time* judgment remained on the mark.

Among Williams's works, none has earned more attention and admiration from critics and scholars or been given more major professional productions than *Streetcar*. The play's 855 Broadway performances between December 1947 and December 1949 make it the longest running of all the dramatist's successes. The highly acclaimed movie version (1951), with Marlon Brando repeating his Broadway triumph as Stanley Kowalski and Vivien Leigh playing Blanche, as she had done on the London stage, was not only hugely successful but something of a landmark film. It demonstrated to Hollywood the possibilities for handling adult subject matter in an artistic way, despite the censor's demand that there be no mention of homosexuality and that Stella ultimately turn away from Stanley. Thirty years later (1984), a new generation would be introduced to Williams's characters in a skillful television adaptation, with Ann-Margret and Treat Williams and directed by John Erman. And Valerie Bettis's balletic version of *A Streetcar Named Desire* (1952), choreographed to music from Alex North's original film score, was seen on public television as recently as 1988. Although the seemingly gentler and more elegiac *The Glass Menagerie* is perhaps held in higher affection by its audiences, the emotional impact of *Streetcar* would appear to be more powerful and longer lasting. The character of Blanche DuBois, as portrayed on stage and screen both here and in England by such actresses as Jessica Tandy, Uta Hagen, Vivien Leigh, Tallulah Bankhead, Claire Bloom, Faye Dunaway, Ann-Margret, and Blythe Danner, is probably the most memorable and widely known of all American dramatic characters and a permanent addition to our nation's cultural mythology: it seems little exaggeration to say that Blanche continues to face virtually no challenge to holding the title as our Oedipus and our Hamlet.

2

The Importance of the Work

In *Precious Sons* (1986), George Furth's family problem play of several seasons ago, the younger boy leaves home to find fame through a minor role in a road show; the play the theatrical troupe is performing is none other than Tennessee Williams's *A Streetcar Named Desire*. Only a handful of works in the history of American drama have entered into and become the property of the public imagination in this way, so that a reference or an allusion to them will prompt an almost instantaneous nod of recognition on the part of audiences and readers. Certainly Thornton Wilder's *Our Town* (1938) and Arthur Miller's *Death of a Salesman* (1949) can be counted among such works. So, too, can *Streetcar*, which, partly because of its justly famous film adaptation, has become an ingredient in our popular mythology, as Furth's use of it attests.

In his autobiographical memoir, *Timebends: A Life* (1987), Miller, the other major dramatist of the post–World War II generation, reports that the experience of seeing *A Streetcar Named Desire* served as a kind of tonic that "strengthened" him in the writing of *Death of a Salesman*. He elaborates that the "one specific door" it threw open was "not the story or characters or direction, but the words and their liberation, the joy of the writer in writing them, the radiant eloquence of its composition, [that] moved me more than all its pathos. It formed a bridge . . . to the whole tradition of unashamed word-joy that . . . we had . . . turned our backs on."[3] Miller rightly senses that one of Williams's chief contributions to the American theater through *Streetcar,* building upon what he had begun in his first great success, *The Glass Menagerie,* was an almost entirely new conception of a lyrical drama; fully utilizing the stylistic possibilities of the stage allowed Williams to break away from the language-bound realistic drama of the nineteenth century that had continued to hold sway in the works of such native playwrights as Eugene O'Neill, Clifford Odets, Robert Sherwood, and Lillian Hellman. This new type of play would not only admit but insist that the language of drama involves more than just words; it would acknowledge the stage symbols and the scenic images that speak to the audience as powerfully as what issues from the mouths of the characters.

Miller discovered in *Streetcar,* then, a map for the way in which the theatrical form could be opened up. Moreover, when it came time to produce *Salesman* on stage, two essential members of the creative team—the director, Elia Kazan, and the scenic and lighting designer, Jo Mielziner—had performed those same roles in the production of *Streetcar;* Mielziner had earlier designed *Menagerie* as well. These collaborators worked toward creating a greater spatial fluidity than the conventions of strict realism traditionally allowed. A realistic play, that is, one at which the audience suspends its disbelief and makes believe that what is on the stage is not a fictional construct but real, was ordinarily performed on a "box set" that creates the illusion of an actual room: three solid walls with an imaginary fourth wall that separates the characters from the audience and through which the spectators peer at the action and overhear the conversation. Such an illusionistic theater asks, in short, that its audience make believe that it is *not* making believe—that it accepts fiction as reality. At the same time, the performers must act as if they are totally oblivious to the presence of an audience beyond the footlights, never acknowledging them. While desirous of maintaining—and even extending through expressionistic devices—the same verisimilitude in characterization that had been the chief hallmark of dramatic realism, Williams (and Miller after him) envisioned a use of theatrical space that would not demand that the spectators deny they are in an auditorium watching a play. Furthermore, the location for the action would not be restricted to any one room, as the dramatist, aided by the designer's use of painted gauze scrims that could be made transparent through lighting, conceived of a freer handling of space, allowing for simultaneous action in different settings, or for showing both the inside and outside of a room, or many rooms.

A further distinction that sets *Streetcar* apart from virtually every American play that preceded it—and from the majority that would follow—is Williams's ability to capture something of the complexity of the novel within the dramatic form, especially in the area of character probity and psychology. In this, he parallels that seminal work in the cinematic medium of the forties, Orson Welles's classic *Citizen Kane* (1941). Although Williams's play does not attempt the structural complexity of Welles's film—whose rotating point of view resembles William Faulkner's use of that technique in *The Sound and the Fury* (1929) or *As I Lay Dying* (1931)—they share density in characterization, a sophistication in the handling of the possibilities of their respective media, and a depth of thematic resonance.

3

Critical Reception

Within a quarter century or so of its first appearance on Broadway, *A Streetcar Named Desire's* status as one of the handful of classic works of American dramatic literature had firmly solidified. In *A Theater Divided* (1967), Martin Gottfried, for example, would rank it along with Miller's *Death of a Salesman* "as one of the two American masterpieces of the postwar years. . . . perhaps the most romantic, poetic and sensitive play ever written for the American theater"; a few years later Jordan Miller would call it quite simply "a work as important as any other ever written for the American stage."[4] The prominent position that *Streetcar* would come to occupy could almost have been guessed, not just from the reviewers' opinions—though these were not unanimous raves without hint of criticism—but especially from the unusual seriousness and care with which they attended to Williams's second success. Finding it a richer and subtler drama than the gentler and more elegiac *The Glass Menagerie* of a few seasons earlier, they generally heaped praise upon every aspect of the production—acting, directing, design—and upon its author, whom they described as a "lyric poet" in prose (the phrase is Joseph Wood Krutch's but the judgment was echoed by others), writing in a mode that fellow playwright and novelist Irwin Shaw termed "heightened naturalism."[5]

What criticisms the early reviewers did register centered on three issues: the potentially shocking nature of Williams's material, the seemingly loose way in which he structured it, and the apparently pessimistic stance he took toward human existence. A fourth, the question of Williams's ambiguous attitude toward his two central characters, what to Brooks Atkinson was the dramatist's refusal to "take sides" and to John Mason Brown a hesitancy to pass "moral judgment"[6] at least on his heroine, was variously recorded on both the credit and debit side of the ledger; Williams undoubtedly considered it a virtue, since in his essays he recurrently praises ambiguity in characterization as one of the hallmarks of great drama. What Richard Watts saw as a deterministic point of view that hopelessly "doomed" the heroine, perhaps Williams saw as a realistic understanding of how pragmatic and utilitarian modes of thinking stand ready to dampen artistic sensitivity and condemn any hint of deviation from societal norms.

The use of a succession of cinematic scenes rather than longer acts prompted a number of early critics, such as Ward Morehouse and Robert Coleman, to conclude that the play's movement was "jerky" and "episodic"; a few others, including Louis Kronenberger, even judged it "somewhat static" and lacking in forward momentum.[7] If Williams had been self-conscious about the potential for audience disorientation over the episodic quality of *The Glass Menagerie*—to the point where he proposed that legends and images be flashed on a screen in the manner of Bertolt Brecht to help them keep their bearings—with *Streetcar* he trusted completely in the directorial skill of Elia Kazan to blunt the episodic structure, to keep it "on the tracks in those dangerous, fast curves it made here and there."[8] Nothing he could do, however, short of totally distorting his vision, could prevent a puritanical reaction against what some saw as an undue emphasis upon the purely sensational elements in the lives of his characters. Even such a normally astute critic as George Jean Nathan, one of the chief proselytizers for Eugene O'Neill's plays, judged

Streetcar "a theatrical shocker" rather than particularly enlightening or spiritually elevating; his demure was mild compared to that of novelist Mary McCarthy, who railed against Williams for capitalizing on "the whole classic paraphernalia of insult and injury" in the search for box-office success.[9]

Each director's interpretation of a playscript is, in a sense, an exercise in critical analysis, and the drama as realized in its initial production thus becomes the first instance of interpretive criticism of the play. Reviewers, then, are commenting not on the text itself as a literary entity but on a single version that is but one of many potential realizations of the text. In the case of *Streetcar*, Kazan's interpretation was available not only in the production as seen on stage, but also in his extensive and extremely enlightening private notebook entries written as he prepared the text for production and later published. In these, he thoroughly analyzes each of the four central figures, attempting to discover what he calls the "spine" that motivates their behavior. He also delineates what he sees as the work's theme ("the crude forces of violence, insensibility and vulgarity" crushing the representative of "light and culture"); its style (a revelation of the "subjective" or "inner life" of a character); its mode ("poetic tragedy"); and the means of maintaining a focus throughout an episodic arrangement of action ("keep each scene in terms of Blanche").[10] In *Against Interpretation* (1966) Susan Sontag takes issue with the way she feels Kazan enforced a meaning upon the text that Williams did not intend; Eric Bentley in *In Search of Theater* (1953) finds that Kazan's direction of Brando as Stanley—which has come to be seen as perhaps the most famous stage performance ever by an American actor—distorted the text by making the "tough talk" of the "brutal" Stanley simply "the mask of a suffering human soul."[11] Even Jessica Tandy, the original Blanche, came to believe that Kazan's initial production was tilted too much toward the "Stanley side of the picture."[12]

That audiences tended to identify strongly with Stanley during the first part of the play, as Kazan intended they would, is one of the points addressed by Harold Clurman, himself a renowned director of the Group Theatre, which, during the thirties and particularly in its presentations of works by Clifford Odets, came as close as perhaps any American theatrical organization ever has to reaching an ideal of ensemble acting. Clurman concluded that because of the directorial conception of Brando's role, "the play becomes the triumph of Stanley Kowalski with the collusion of the audience." Indeed, Clurman's seminal essay review, which sagely recognizes that Williams's "beautiful" and "original" work "stands very high among the creative contributions of the American theatre since 1920" and ranks "among the few worthy of a permanent place" in our national repertory, catalogs virtually all of the issues that have since concerned critics and scholars: Williams's thematic emphasis "that aspiration, sensitivity, departure from the norm are battered, bruised and disgraced in our world today"; Blanche's characterization as an artist figure, both flawed and victimized, and the necessity for audiences to be convinced of "the soundness of her values"; and finally Stanley's role as a brutish, energetic "unwitting antichrist of our time, the little man who will break the back of every effort to create a more comprehensive world in which thought and conscience, a broader humanity are expected to evolve from the old Adam."[13]

Within less than a decade and a half of the initial reviews, the high position and continued importance of *Streetcar* as an American literary/dramatic text was signaled by the publication of John Hurrell's *Two Modern American Tragedies: Reviews and Criticism of "Death of a Salesman" and "A Streetcar Named Desire"* (1961). If Hurrell's title begged the question of whether or not—and, if so, in what ways— Williams's play might be considered an example of tragic drama, Jordan Miller's introduction to *Twentieth Century Interpretations of "A Streetcar Named Desire"* (1971), a collection whose weight and substance reflect ten additional years of commentary, approaches the issue head-on. Because of Blanche's "defiant courage" in the face of an inevitable defeat brought about by "trying to survive with some shred of human dignity" in an inhospitable and even hostile world, the audience experiences, according to Miller, a sense of "tragic waste" that brings *Streetcar* "as close to genuine tragedy as any modern American drama."[14]

Although scholars such as Mary Ann Corrigan, Bert Cardullo, and Henry Schvey have, over the years, expertly addressed *Streetcar*'s stylistic devices and visual imagery, in the interval between Clurman's lengthy review and now, the majority of the most substantial articles (those by Leonard Berkman and Leonard Quarino, among others) have focused on the plight of the play's heroine. Moreover, with the eighties have come a number of specifically feminist approaches, most notably in studies by Kathleen Hulley and Avea Vlasopolos. Hulley's semiotic reading of the text sees the two central figures in the play as writing and directing mutually exclusive theatrical texts that the other characters (and the audience) must then choose between: to privilege Stanley's text over Blanche's is to exclude everything in life "which makes art and love possible."[15] Vlasopolos's argument follows somewhat similar lines but focuses more specifically on the realm of language: Stanley's factual "language of power," though "impoverished," embodies "the dominant discourse of patriarchy." Blanche poses a threat to his "interpretive authority" by actions that are subversive of the traditional social order that victimizes and tries to render her powerless. She finally submits to another authority, this one scientific, represented by the male psychiatrist.[16]

Two of the most worthwhile book chapters on *Streetcar,* separated by twenty years, offer quite diverse mythic readings of the work, one cultural, the other classical. In *Myth and Modern American Drama* (1969) Thomas Porter focuses on Williams's handling of the dying out of the Old South through his character study of Blanche, who is both the alien "intruder" upon an "established way of life" as well as the traditional "heroine of romance." This tension is further exacerbated by the playwright's ambivalence about sex, which, to Porter's way of thinking, helps account for the play's final lack of resolution, with Williams's "Southerner . . . caught between two worlds, one gone with the wind, the other barely worth having."[17] More recently, in *Tennessee Williams's Plays: Memory, Myth and Symbol* (1987), Judith Thompson examines in great detail allusions to classical, literary, and biblical mythology. She discovers analogues for Blanche in Persephone, Psyche, Delilah, and Camille, and for Stanley in Dionysus; and because a curse seems to have befallen the DuBois ancestral house, a once Edenic spot has been lost and the golden age has degenerated. Any inclusive reading of *Streetcar* will necessarily confront many of the issues raised by the earliest critics of Williams's masterwork and carried on by their successors.

A Reading

Manuscript page showing the play's change in title in Tennessee Williams's hand.
Reproduced by permission of the Harry Ransom Humanities Research Center Library, University of Texas at Austin.

4

The Structure

"I'm only passing through"

Like Williams's *The Glass Menagerie* of a few years earlier and his *Camino Real* of several years later, *A Streetcar Named Desire* is an episodic drama comprised of a number of scenes (eleven), some of which (such as scene 5) might almost stand alone as little plays. Unlike either *Menagerie* or *Camino*, however, *Streetcar* does not employ a narrator to bridge the scenes or interpolate for the audience—not that such bridging is in any way necessary. In performance, in fact, *Streetcar* easily adapts itself to the three-act structure common to the commercial theater of its day (two acts are more normal now), with rather natural breaks occurring after scenes 4 and 6. These points mark shifts in the seasons: from the late spring of scenes 1 through 4 to the late summer in scenes 5 and 6 and the very early fall in scenes 7 through 11. The word *Streetcar* in Williams's title points, of course, to a mode of transportation. Blanche's opening line about disembarking from a series of such conveyances introduces the notion of a journey. Virtually her last line in the play, "I'm only passing through (173)," concludes the metaphor and confirms the spectators' sense that Williams builds his action around the image of an alienated, isolated wanderer seeking some kind of human connection.

In scene 1, Williams presents his newly arrived heroine's attempts to form a bond both with—and in the face of—all of the other communities or relationships present on the stage: Stanley and Stella's marriage; Stanley and his beer-drinking bowling partners (here represented initially by Mitch and later by Steve); Eunice and the Negro Woman, and then Eunice and Stella, who suggest the possibility—indeed, the necessity—that women who live primarily in the shadow of their husbands forge bonds of support among themselves. Blanche's bonds in the past, at least those the audience learns of early in the play, have been with family, all of whom, except for Stella, are now dead. Yet when she comes as an outsider to Stella and Stanley's home and "community," Blanche is so frightened of rejection and desperately unsure of herself that she inadvertently makes herself generally unwelcome, acting almost rudely to Eunice and being condescending to and demanding of Stella.

By scene 2 Stella and Blanche have reached a rapprochement that makes it appear as though the sisterly bond might be reestablished. But fear of losing his place were this to occur now makes Stanley feel like an outsider and puts him on the defensive. A man to whom much has been denied, he must cover over any inadequacy by bullying and constantly competing, so he can always come out on top. Blanche's deepest bond from the past is hinted at when Stanley, deficient in understanding the things of the heart, dirties the poems from the dead youth by scattering them on the floor; nevertheless, once Blanche recoups, she holds her own with her brother-in-law over the question of Belle Reve's loss. The scene can end with the sisters restored to one another, yet the final image of Stella leading Blanche away as the poker players arrive points uneasily forward to the play's end, when Blanche is taken away, severed from any close connection with a fellow human being.

Scene 3, entitled "The Poker Night," presents the most assured community in the play, an example of male bonding replete with its own rituals and total exclusion of women. Mitch, however, distances himself somewhat from his male cohorts, and Blanche confirms this, immediately differentiating him from the others by virtue of his sensitivity. They share, as well, the loss of a loved one through death. As Blanche and Mitch tentatively move toward one another, Stanley's macho display of his volatile physicality causes a rupture with Stella, so that his separateness is momentarily accentuated. Very quickly, though, his submissiveness, as of a child to its mother, not only wins her back but sweeps her off her feet; she is in his thrall once more. The kindness that Blanche needs and that Mitch proffers is simultaneously undercut in a foreboding manner by his sympathetic attitude toward the relationship between Stanley and Stella; the thread binding Blanche to Mitch is tenuous at best. Scene 4 finds Stella reconfirming her total allegiance to Stanley: not only does she make excuses for his behavior, however violent and demeaning, but she defiantly rejects Blanche's assessment of his commonness and her attempts to valorize things of the spirit. She "fiercely" embraces Stanley, who "grins" in triumph over Blanche's total exclusion.

Blanche attempts to assuage her aloneness early in scene 5 by resorting to an imaginative recall of her old beau Shep Huntleigh—a relationship whose importance has been distorted by the passage of time and memory's tendency to embroider. In her first real moment of communication with Stella, Blanche suggests that the passing of time and her resulting decreasing allure is perhaps her major impediment to forming a permanent bond. Stanley's arrival shortens the conversation, and, when left alone, Blanche makes overtures designed to seduce the young paperboy; even while resisting the temptation, she reveals how she satisfied desire after the death of her husband. That she depends upon illusion to build and sustain any relationship with Mitch becomes clear when she demands he act as Mr. Rosenkavalier come to court her. The strain carries over to the beginning of scene 6 when she comments that society's expectations that a woman entice a man, yet not be too forward, constrict the natural expression of feeling. She realizes that she has "overstayed" her welcome at the Kowalskis', yet sensing that she has won over Mitch she can now be more forward. The scene ends with her confession of how she broke the bond of connectedness with her husband through her failure to be lovingly and nonjudgmentally compassionate—a confession that allows Mitch and Blanche to huddle together in mutual need. Blanche feels saved, as secure as she will ever feel—and whatever reservations the audience might have had over giving her their complete sympathy evaporate.

The dramatic irony arising in scene 7 when the audience learns (with Blanche offstage) that Stanley has thwarted any permanent coming together of Mitch and Blanche in marriage therefore becomes intensely painful. By revealing that, through a misplaced sense of duty to his friend, he has broken down Mitch's belief in Blanche's worthiness as an object for his love, Stanley takes a calculated risk that Stella's natural recoiling from him will be only temporary; and, indeed, in the next scene he moves to restore things to the way they were before Blanche's arrival, once again defying Stella to choose him over her sister. The birthday celebration gone awry in scene 8 (with Mitch's absence conspicuous because of the empty space at the festively decorated table) ends with the announcement that Stella is going into labor: now, certainly no place remains for Blanche. Yet despite Stanley's suddenly solicitous attitude toward his wife, there is more than a hint that the baby's arrival might be just as disruptive to his relationship with Stella as Blanche's has been.

Scenes 9 and 10—significantly, the only scenes with just two characters on stage—must be seen as a pair, with Mitch's actions in the former different in degree though not in kind from Stanley's in the latter. In both, Blanche's final condition of aloneness is sealed. The destructiveness of Mitch's violation of Blanche's right to dignity by subjecting her to the merciless glare of the naked light bulb is underscored by the appearance of the woman peddling flowers for the dead, which Blanche senses are somehow meant for her. Mitch's attempt, then, to force himself upon her as if she deserved nothing more than to be sexually used is an assault before the rape in scene 10. Abruptly brought back from her protective retreat into the past at the beginning of the scene to face the man she calls her "executioner," Blanche knows that any hope now of establishing a saving relationship with another human being is lost. Ironically, Stanley uses the act that should consecrate the most intimate and binding of unions to sever Blanche permanently from any possibility of physical connectedness with another. Her journey from loneliness to an even more intense and final aloneness is what the play charts.

At the close of the play in scene 11, the three communities that were present in scene 1 are onstage once again, under the same turquoise blue sky that symbolizes a once pristine world now lost and not to be found because not earthly. The men sit at their poker game one more time; the women renew their functions as emotional support for one another; the family now has a child. Not that Blanche's transitory presence has been without impact upon each of these groups: Stanley must forcibly restrain Mitch from leaving the poker table and entering Blanche's world to come to her aid; Stella, though she turns to Eunice's arms for comfort, still doubts Eunice's counsel that she had no choice but to believe Stanley's lie rather than admit Blanche's truth about the rape; and the marriage will be colored both by Stella's suspicions about Stanley as well as by her lessened dependence upon him for emotional support and her attachment to the child. Furthermore, the opportunity that existed for bonding between Williams's two sisters at the play's beginning goes unrealized at the end as Blanche does not respond to Stella's cries. Blanche exits, led away as if blind (as she had been by Stella at the close of scene 2) to the asylum; though "kindness," ironically, might exist there at the hands of "strangers," the more potent message is that the solitary Blanche will be able to create at best only the illusion of human interconnectedness through the power of the imagination to defy the reality of separateness. This pattern of bonds between people maimed and broken functions as Williams's chief structural device, a pattern that finally becomes powerfully thematic.

The Stage Setting

An especially important avenue into a play for any reader or spectator is careful attention to the clues the dramatist provides in his or her setting before the characters even enter the scene, and then in the entrance of the central characters. As the theater critic and director Robert Brustein remarked, "When the lights go up on a play, you are entering a designer's world, and it is the designer's images that plant themselves indelibly on the edge of your mind."[18] The spectators at Williams's *A Streetcar Named Desire* would first see, in Jo Mielziner's rendition of the dramatist's stage description, the exterior of a corner apartment on a street in the French Quarter of New Orleans ironically called Elysian Fields after the blissful mythological region where the souls of the blessed and of the much touted heroes reside. It is early May, and the sky in the background "*is a peculiarly tender blue, almost a turquois*" (3), the color of some remembered innocent Eden; when the play ends, it will be mid-September under a sky of the same tone. The seasonal movement is thus from late spring to early fall, from promise of regeneration and renewal to (potentially) fruitful harvest followed by certain decline. The street, Williams specifies, "*runs between the L&N tracks and the river*," that is, it is bounded by the famed river god of old that once transported people and goods westward into the promised land and the newer, mechanized means of transportation associated with the captains of the industrial age and their getting and keeping that ultimately lay waste.

The two-flat building on Elysian Fields that houses the Kowalskis and their upstairs neighbors, the Hubbels, partakes of that same mix of old and new, of tradition and grace wearing down. Now "*weathered grey*" with "*faded white stairs*" and "*rickety . . . galleries* (3)," it still retains enough architectural touches from the past—the "*quaintly ornamented gables*," for instance—to evoke the decaying condition of Belle Reve (French for "beautiful dream"), the old DuBois ancestral home, which symbolizes the cavalier South in decline. When the lights fade on the gauzy, shimmery exterior and rise on the inside two rooms of the apartment, the contrast from beauty—even beauty in decay—is startling. Here the colors, though still dingy with age, are primary, greens and yellows, rather than muted—a fitting reflection, like the spirited yet sometimes dissonant jazz music (the recurrent blue piano, trumpet, and drums heard during the play) of the wilder side of the Quarter. Blanche tries to make a comfortable niche for herself in this alien world by adding a patina of the old grace to her makeshift bedroom with its curtain divider. In her highly anxious condition the territory outside the apartment recalls "the ghoul–haunted woodland of Weir" (12), where the persona in Poe's poem had interred his beloved Ulalume—an apt allusion about lost loves in both the past and future. With the street cries of the vendors and the easy camaraderie between the races, the Quarter is an exuberant, unceremonious, and unembarrassed world in which Stanley, predictably, is perfectly at home.

The Characters' Entrances

Whereas his later adaptation of *Streetcar* for the screen opens (after the establishing shots) with Blanche's arrival, in the play Williams briefly brings on Stanley first but only to have him leave almost as soon as he has entered. While this strategy builds on the convention whereby the appearance of a play's protagonist is delayed to heighten audience expectation, here the technique primarily serves to define those aspects of the setting that will make this milieu hostile to Blanche and to sketch a vibrant first impression of her adversary. For Stanley *belongs* in the Quarter; its open and unpretentious style and its gutsy and sizzling life become him. Dressed in the denim clothes and bowling jacket of the middle-class workman, he struts in as the macho owner and controller of the scene, "*bellowing*" at the top of his lungs for his wife, Stella. He throws her a blood-stained package of meat from the butchers—an action that vulgarly announces his manhood and his pride in it. The *onstage* audience—his fawning wife, Stella, feigning disapproval while actually rather "thrilled" over such displays by her husband, and their two neighbor women, one black, the other white—all laugh joyously at the performance; their response serves simultaneouly as a signal and a measure of the theater audience's own. Yet the onstage as well as the offstage spectators, initially swept up by Stanley's self-assuredness and easy, if sexist, good humor, will be visited momentarily by a lost and dazed lady from another world entirely who can only be horrified by Stanley—and by any audience's permissive and uncritical acceptance of him.

If Stanley enters in power and glory, Blanche arrives in New Orleans from Belle Reve wan and defenseless. Her almost unmannerly curtness and her refusal to enter into the continual party that is typical of life in the Quarter immediately cost her the approval of one member of the onstage audience, the upstairs tenant Eunice; in this instance, however, it is a lack of sympathy that the spectators in the theater who sense Blanche's desperation would do well not to share. "*Incongruous[ly and] daintily dressed*" (5) for this boisterous and raunchy section of the Quarter, Blanche is out of place and ill at ease not only because of her demeanor and refinement, but because of her highly strung emotional and psychological state as well. Next to Stanley's swaggering virility, she is the frightened, nearly hysterical "*moth*" seeking protection and safety. An emissary from a past world of plantations and "white columns," at this point she poses no threat to Stanley and Stella's world, which has its own rules of behavior far different from hers. Rather, devoid of inner reserves, she is at their mercy.

The pattern of arrival and departure is a recurrent one in drama. Blanche has endured much trauma before her entrance, but she comes hoping that the trauma is past, and that salvation of some kind awaits her. What lies before her is not a search for enlightenment or self-knowledge, since she has already fully experienced her own guilt and responsibility in reaching her present condition. Yet she could hardly expect the punishment and destruction that await her at the hands of her antagonist, somewhat unwittingly abetted even by those whose innate sensibilities are similar to her own and who should thus act as her protectors.

5

The Style

"A new, plastic theatre"

Tom Wingfield, the authorial character/narrator of *The Glass Menagerie*, opens the play by drawing a theoretical distinction between traditional realistic drama, which "gives you illusion that has the appearance of truth," and what has come to be called Williams's "theater of gauze," which plays unabashedly with the conventions of the stage, makes the audience more self-conscious of the playgoing experience, and thus gives "truth in the pleasant disguise of illusion."[19] The aim is not to distract us from the essential truth of experience but to take us deeper into it through all of the sensuous means—not simply words, but lighting, music, color, sound—available to the writer. These kinesthetic effects, though more often associated with works by painters, sculptors, and choreographers, are available as well to dramatists as tools in the creation of the aesthetic object. As Williams writes in his afterword to *Camino Real* (1953), "I feel, as the painter did, that the messages lie in those abstract beauties of form and color and line, to which I would add light and motion" (*Essays*, 69).

In his production notes to *Menagerie*—an important critical manifesto calling for "a new, plastic theatre which must take the place of the exhausted theatre of realistic conventions (7)"—Williams expands upon Tom Wingfield's notion of a nonillusionistic drama that aims to plumb the truths of existence rather than to provide an exact representation of reality: "When a play employs unconventional techniques, it is not, or certainly shouldn't be, trying to escape its responsibility of dealing with reality, or interpreting experience, but is actually or should be attempting to find a closer approach, a more penetrating and vivid expression of things as they are (7)." And this penetration of reality that Williams calls for can best be attained by a perspective that is poetic in the broad sense, one that does not restrict itself to the verbal but incorporates the visual and the tactile too: "Truth, life, or reality is an organic thing which the poetic imagination can represent or suggest, in essence, only through transformation, through changing into other forms than those which were merely present in appearance (7)." It is more than lyrical language, or even recurrent scenic images of great visual beauty, that justify terming Williams a "poetic dramatist"; it is a habit of seeing experience as a multilayered construct or network that tends toward the metaphoric, the symbolic, the archetypal.

Expressionism

The one methodology Williams specifically mentions in his production notes that employs "unconventional techniques" to effect "a closer approach to truth" is expressionism. As a movement that embraced, especially in the early years of this century, not only drama but the other pictorial arts of painting, sculpture, and cinema as well, expressionism has as its goal the objectification of the *inner* experience of reality. Through a heavy dependence upon symbols, it attempts to transform into something ascertainable by the senses the interior or psychic condition of—in the case of drama—the central character onstage. Williams finds this potentiality of expressionism, rather than its sometimes explicit criticism of a dehumanizing technological society or its tendency toward allegory, particularly fruitful in his characterization of Blanche DuBois (Miller later does, too, with Willy Loman in *Salesman*). It allows him to express through visual rather than verbal means what is going on in the mind of his protagonist, and even the nightmarish disintegration of that mind.

A *Streetcar Named Desire* is most expressionistic precisely at those moments when the audience shares with Blanche an internal perception that is not apparent to the other characters. Similar to the use of the Narrator in *Menagerie*, this approach approximates in drama the first person limited point of view used in fiction. The viewer sees and hears along with Blanche such disturbing and disorienting images and sounds as the screeching of the cat, the glare of the locomotive lights, the music of the Varsouviana polka and the gunshot noise that silences it, the menacing reflections and shadows that appear on the walls, and the inhuman voices and echoes that help replicate her mental state at the end of the play. The play, in fact, becomes more expressionistic in its style as Blanche's emotional and mental breakdown becomes more pronounced. What in the older, word-bound drama would be talked about Williams conveys through means previously employed mainly by the plastic artist.

Symbolism

Despite their usefulness in objectifying what is essentially subjective, symbols are not, of course, the exclusive domain of the expressionistic movement; as Tom Driver remarks, it has always been a natural tendency of the stage to turn things into symbols. And symbols are, as Williams makes abundantly clear in his essays over the years, an integral part of his dramatic technique; he ventures to say, and not at all facetiously, that "without my symbols I might still be employed by the International Shoe Co. in St. Louis" (*Essays*, 142). Claiming that all "art is made out of symbols the way your body is made out of vital tissue," and that any "play that is more of a dramatic poem than a play is bound to rest on metaphorical ways of expression" (*Essays*,

146), Williams concludes, this time in his foreword to *Camino Real*, that "symbols are nothing but the natural speech of drama . . . the purest language of plays" (*Essays*, 66) Arguing, in a fashion similar to Carl Jung, that everyone's mind is an immense reservoir of shared images on which both dreams and communication are based, Williams claims the chief purpose of symbolism in drama is "say[ing] a thing more directly and simply and beautifully than it could be said in words. . . . Sometimes it would take page after tedious page of exposition to put across an idea that can be said with an object or a gesture on the lighted stage" (*Essays*, 66).

Williams structures *Streetcar* using a vast network of imagery arranged in patterns of opposition. Tracing how Williams employs a major—perhaps *the* major—symbol in his play provides insight into his approach. Blanche, hypersensitive to her declining physical beauty, cannot tolerate being seen in bright light. She covers over the harsh glare of reality with a patina of illusion that shows her off under a favorable glow. And so, when she sees the naked light bulb in Stanley and Stella's bedroom, she buys a delicately painted Chinese lantern to soften the glare. Blanche's condition is as fragile—physically, psychologically, emotionally—as the easily destructible paper lantern: the lantern becomes not only a symbol of her vulnerability and subjugation to time's decay, but also a symbol for the imaginative or creative act that at least temporarily protects her from the grimness and cruelty of reality. When Mitch and, later, Stanley tear the lantern off the bulb, it is as if they are attacking Blanche herself and destroying her world of illusion/art. For Blanche there exists an order higher than what is merely factually true, whereas for Stanley the merciless light of unvarnished reality, exposing everything for what it is, is the only truth he can or will recognize.

The Protagonists' Images

Williams's ever-expanding framework of visual and verbal imagery encompasses not only specific objects that become symbolic but also more abstract notions that echo and reecho in the characters' speeches. Stanley and Blanche need only come onto the stage for the process of constructing meaning through imagery to begin.

Blanche is like an apparition in white, and she continues to wear soft materials in pastel shades throughout most of the play. The white suggests the purity (her astrological sign is Virgo) that she desires to restore: she uses hot baths to calm her frazzled nerves and purify her spirit and hopes the cleansing bright blue sea will receive her in death. What surrounds her must be soft and soothing: the harsh glare of the naked light bulb that reveals the ravages of time to others—as the reflection from the hand mirror does to Blanche herself—must be muted by the Chinese lantern; for her music, she replaces the romantic refrain of the Varsouviana polka, now horrible to her ears because of its associations with her dead husband, with the "pure" cathedral bells. In her fragility she is mothlike, a creature of soul, yet easily victimized.

Blanche is, however, also tigress and seductress, as her red satin robe denotes. Her inability to accept the coexistence of these opposite inclinations is at the root of her psychic difficulties. Blanche wants desperately to be a creature of culture, refinement, and gentility. She uses her poetic and imaginative faculties to re-create a charmed world, but Belle Reve and the idealized South that it stands for is only a "beautiful dream," long a thing of the past, if it ever existed at all. Its beauty has declined; its moral blindness has led to decadence; the guilt from the horror of slavery on which the plantation system was built and thrived has sapped its strength.

Yet if Blanche's nostalgic dream of the past can be so limiting that it circumscribes the present, a present like Stanley's that is totally devoid of roots in the past can be emptied of all moral and physical beauty. Stanley's universe thrives on bold, bright colors—the green and scarlet bowling shirts, the red silk pajamas, the colored lights of sexuality—that help parade and show off his pure physicality and animality (his astrological sign is Capricorn, the goat). The pulsating rhythms of jazz, the blue piano and trumpet and drums, are his, as is the cold shower that does little to dampen his lust. He is the cruel victimizer and executioner of Blanche's moth, the weak and unsuspecting intruder. Crude jokes and vulgar behavior, beer and poker parties replace poetry in his world of facts, a practical universe in which fantasies are only destructive lies that have no potential for revealing truths of the heart and spirit. Although living now in New Orleans, Stanley, from immigrant stock, is a creature of the North; as a traveler peddling products from a factory assembly line, he represents an urbanized, mechanized culture that measures the value of a thing only by its material usefulness. The worlds that Stanley and Blanche inhabit and symbolize could hardly be more diametrically opposed.

A Fragmented Universe

Although to do so involves simplification, the two worlds of Stanley and Blanche can be charted as a vast and complex network of antinomies. This pattern expands as the play proceeds; Williams imbues it with increasing thematic resonance.

Stanley	*Blanche*
Desire (Eros)	Death (Thanatos)
brightly colored silks	whites and pastels
colored lights, naked bulb	paper lantern, candle
jazz (piano, drums, trumpet)	polka and cathedral bells
cold showers	hot baths
predator	moth
masculine virility	feminine fragility
Capricorn	Virgo
crudeness, vulgarity	gentility, refinement
victimizer, executioner	victim
cruelty, violence, brutality	kindness
poker	poetry
facts	imagination, fantasy
body, corporeality, matter	soul, spirit
sanity, rationality	lunacy, imbalance
strength, on the rise	decadence, decline

The Style

mechanization, usefulness	beauty
locomotive	streetcar
commonness	culture, pretension
North	South
the city (New Orleans)	the country (Belle Reve)

Through this extensive system of dichotomies, Williams makes his thematic point that to fragment or dissociate human experience by seeing it as a mutually exclusive, either/or series of options, rather than to regard it from an integrative, both/and perspective, is one of our greatest sins, debilitating both to the individual and to society. To set up and live by such a Manichaean dualism—one, for instance, that claims sexuality is always brutalization and can never become salvation, that the bestial cannot exist alongside the beautiful, or that only reality and never fantasy can be true and life-giving—is to deny humankind's condition as creatures of the Fall who have been redeemed, and thus to invite emotional and psychic imbalance and disorder.

6

Blanche

In one of her most famous essays, "Mr. Bennett and Mrs. Brown," the twentieth-century British novelist Virginia Woolf speculates that "men and women write novels because they are lured on to create some character which has . . . imposed itself upon them. . . . The study of character becomes to them an absorbing pursuit; to impart character an obsession." She adds that what readers most recall about a great book is "some character who . . . has the power to make you think not merely of itself, but of all sorts of things through its eyes."[20] What Woolf says about novelists and their readers applies equally well to playwrights and their audiences. C. W. E. Bigsby, a British scholar who has become one of the most perceptive contemporary critics of modern American drama, remarks on the centrality of "character" in any discussion of drama: "It is offered as definitional of a genre that, whatever its mystical or epic origins, has become a primary expression of bourgeois individualism. Theatre, in its modern form, is seen as an art in which characters are the agents of empathetic response, figures by means of which we are drawn to acknowledge the analogical powers of the theatre."[21]

In virtually all of Tennessee Williams's plays, delineating and prob-ing character psychology takes precedence over discussing and arguing philosophical issues; he could be echoing Woolf when he claims that the "chief aim in playwriting is the creation of characters" (*Essays*, 116). In his essay "Critic Says 'Evasion,' Writer Says 'Mystery,' " Williams goes as far as to proclaim: "My characters make my play. . . . I always start with them, they take spirit and body in my mind. . . . They build the play about them like spiders weaving their webs, sea creatures making their shells."[22] Many of Williams's best plays, including *The Glass Menagerie, A Streetcar Named Desire, Summer and Smoke, Cat on a Hot Tin Roof,* and *The Night of the Iguana,* feature multiple protagonists. In the same essay he reproduces a reflective passage from the stage directions in *Cat* that clarifies both his method and his intention as regards character portrayal: "The bird that I hope to catch in the net of this play is not the solution of one man's psychological problem. I'm trying to catch the true quality of experience in a group of people, that cloudy, flickering, evanescent—fiercely charged!—interplay of live human beings in a thundercloud of a common crisis. Some mystery should be left in the revelation of character in a play, just as a great deal of mystery is always left in the revelation of character in life, even in one's own character to himself" (*Essays*, 71–72). Character "interplay" and character "mystery" or ambiguity become hallmarks of Williams's achievement in *Streetcar*.

The Heroine as Role-Player

Williams's characterization of Stanley at the opening of *A Streetcar Named Desire* and the audience's partiality toward his liveliness and vital sense of fun must not blind them to the realization that this *is* Blanche's play. Support for this position comes not only from the provisional title phrase "Blanche's Chair in the Moon" that initially jogged Williams's imagination into the creation of the work, but also from Elia Kazan's intuition and then conviction as the play's director that he should envision each of the eleven scenes as a step in Blanche's progression from arrival to expulsion. According to the director's production "Notebook," Blanche comes to her sister Stella as her last chance for acceptance. Searching to find a "place" where she can belong, she is once more "excluded" as an outsider (scenes 1–3 [365]). From among those who might be expected to welcome and receive her, she discovers that her brother-in-law Stanley immediately sizes her up as an "enemy," a response that her own manner and actions help elicit. But then Blanche thinks she has found in his card-playing buddy Mitch the "perfect" match for her (scenes 4–6). This possibility proves short-lived as Mitch deserts her (scene 7). She believes that "telling the whole truth" about her past might save her, yet is rejected for doing so and "escapes" into a world of illusion ("Notebook," 366). Then Stanley jolts her back into reality and destroys her (scenes 8, 9, and 10). Finally, Blanche "is disposed of," expelled from the world she had entered with such fragile hope at the beginning (scene 11).

At the same time that Kazan charts the protagonist's movement from opening to close, he suggests that Blanche continually adopts a succession of shifting social roles or masks, though his notes do not specify explicitly what each of these is. As Stanley remarks, she "put[s] on her act." To follow her progressive masking and unmasking is to see Blanche playing the demure lady, offended by any open display of sensuality (scene 1), the carefree flirt (Kazan's "Gay Miss Devil-may-care" ["Notebook," 369] of scene 2), the more determined seductress (scene 3). By scenes 4 and 5 the challenge to her role as self-appointed champion of the values threatened by Stanley, who embodies the forces of mechanistic civilization, begins to crack her fragile facade affecting culture and moral superiority. When her carefully staged act balancing shy temptress and demure woman of high ideals succeeds in winning Mitch's heart and offers some promise of salvation at the end of scene 6, she can for the first time finally discard all role-playing during her brief appearance in scene 7. After Mitch fails to show up for her birthday party in scene 8, however, Blanche must revert to the role of the rejected maiden. When that fails to bring a suitably repentant suitor to her door in scene 9, she enters ever deeper, in the last two scenes of the play, into her fantasy about an old beau, Shep Huntleigh, who comes to court her. Her inability to totally erase the reality and lose herself in this illusion partly accounts for the measure of pain the audience feels at her departure.

The Artist/Illusionist

When Blanche leaves her home in Belle Reve for New Orleans, she hopes to erase the past and erect a more promising future. This movement through physical space is symbolic of another route of escape, the flight from harsh reality to fantasy in the landscape of the mind: the lantern, the painted artifact that symbolizes the imaginative faculty, is placed over the glare of the light, shading and redefining it. When Mitch defies her in scene 9, as Stanley does, to give over her deceit and face the facts, unvarnished and unadulterated, Blanche replies in words that help define her (and Williams's) artistic credo: "I don't want realism. I want magic! . . . I try to give that to people. I misrepresent things to them. I don't tell truth, I tell what *ought* to be truth. And if that is sinful, then let me be damned for it!" (145). Sometimes, therefore, what Williams in the production notes to *The Glass Menagerie* terms "photographic likeness" (7) must give way before a higher allegiance to human experience—what the Narrator in *Menagerie* calls "truth in the pleasant disguise of illusion" (22); an awareness of this moral and ethical dimension in art informs Blanche's character and actions in *Streetcar*.

From one perspective, Blanche is as an actress portraying the central character in a play that she first authors and then produces and directs. She treats the Kowalskis' apartment as her theater, altering the decor to make it "almost dainty" (104); their bedroom, separated from the other room by a curtain, becomes the stage for her illusions, with the bathroom serving as an offstage locale. When positioned on the other side of the curtain, Blanche becomes audience/voyeur, both puritanically repelled and enviously fascinated by Stanley and Stella's earthy relationship. When Mitch joins her at the flat after their disappointing evening on Lake Pontchartrain, she becomes the set decorator, lighting a candle in a wine bottle to foster the make-believe that they are sitting in a romantic bohemian café on the Parisian Left Bank—even that they are Camille and Armand from Alexander Dumas's famous play named after its heroine. "Only make-believe," becomes something of Blanche's motto: she repeats it in the refrain of the song she jauntily sings in scene 7 when, not knowing that Stanley has uncovered her sordid past and revealed it to Mitch, she feels secure in the latter's attraction. But make-believe, which transforms the "phony . . . Barnum and Bailey world" with its "honky-tonk parade" and "melody played / In a penny arcade," depends, like all art, on the auditors or spectators giving their willing assent to the creative act of the artist: they, too, must suspend disbelief and commit themselves to the truth of "a paper moon, / Sailing over a cardboard sea" (120–21). Her song becomes the plea, the plaintive lament, that every artist at one time or another makes.

As the central character in a play of her own devising, Blanche carries her own costume and props in her trunk, including the makeup powder and the "gossamer scarf" that cause her to "shimmer and glow." In scene 2, Stanley discovers the "rhinestone tiara she wore to a costume ball" (35). A somewhat drunken Blanche dons the tiara at the opening of scene 10 to crown her "*soiled and crumpled white satin evening gown and a pair of scuffed silver slippers with brilliants set in their heels.*" Talking "*as if to a group of spectral admirers*" (151), she is temporarily lost in an illusion of the past. Yet her self-theatricalization is only successful as long as the illusion is not examined too closely. When she inspects herself in the hand mirror, reality breaks through; no longer able to believe in her own fantasy, "*she slams the mirror face down with such violence that the glass cracks*" (151). By pulling Blanche back from absolute faith in illusion's power to serve as a shield and an escape from the present threatening reality (Stanley's return from the hospital by way of a bar), Williams presages the final scene when reality again breaks through. Blanche realizes that the doctor from the sanatorium is "not the gentleman [she] was expecting" (173)—not the courtier of her romantic dreams come to whisk her safely away from a house built on lies and treachery and deceit fomented by an "executioner" who expels Blanche and her truth.

The Chekhovian Matrix

When Blanche dresses in her faded ball gown and tiara at the beginning of scene 10—a flight of fancy that immediately precedes the most prosaic and brutally literal of the degradations (the rape)—she is the aging southern belle trying to recapture a time now past. As such, she is both an individual and a representative of her society, an emblem of a lost tradition. In Kazan's words, "All her behavior patterns are those of the dying civilization she represents" ("Notebook," 365). In charting the decline not only of very real characters but of an entire civilization, Williams is literary heir to the influential Russian master, Anton Chekhov. In scene 3, when Blanche explains the meaning of her name to Mitch, Williams alludes to the central symbol of one of Chekhov's most famous dramas *The Cherry Orchard* (1904): DuBois "means woods and Blanche means white, so the two together mean white woods. Like an orchard in spring!" (59). Moreover, the seasonal time frames of the two works (May to September in *Streetcar* and May to October in *Orchard*) are analogous. Also, both plays are patterned on the arrival and then departure in defeat of a powerless, hypersensitive woman with a sexual past, and both include a family estate falling into disuse. Chekhov, furthermore, sets up oppositions and dichotomies in much the same way that Williams later does: between a dying out aristocracy fallen prey to a debilitating ennui and an energetic and productive, if somewhat destructive, rising bourgeoisie; between the beauty, culture, and grace of the old and an increasingly utilitarian new. In short, Chekhov composes a swan song for a moribund civilization that both does and does not deserve its fate at the hands of the new vital, albeit ruthless, entrepreneurs. As a moral observer, Chekhov regrets the loss of certain values; still, he understands that fault does not belong to only one side in the struggle.

Williams shares with Chekhov his elegiac, lyrical tone as well as his sense of history and sorrow over a disintegrating, anachronistic tradition. For Williams, as for Chekhov, the concept of loss is key. The once-thriving social and economic system featuring white-columned mansions peopled by landed gentry is no more, and so Blanche is reduced to a servant changing bloody pillowcases on an increasingly empty plantation. When one remembers that Stanley lives principally by and for the physical pleasures of the body, Belle Reve's loss by "the epic fornications" of the DuBois ancestors is significant. Yet Blanche remains prisoner to the traditional notions about women of the old cavalier South: economic dependency was the order of the day, and so women like Blanche were ill-equipped to survive in a changing world by any means *except* physical attractiveness. Blanche attempts to use her fading good looks to win the hand of a charming suitor, eventually latching on to the romantically idealized Shep Huntleigh, who is attainable only in the realm of fantasy. Blanche must maintain a proper balance, being "gay" enough to entertain and entice the gentleman caller without being so sexually forward as to turn him away. Affecting charm and manners, she pathetically tries to keep alive a way of life that has been lost. It is still entrenched, however, in the public imagination by works such as *Gone With the Wind* that mythicize the South's beauty, civilization, and grace, at the expense of its expediency and the barbarousness of the base institution of slavery on which it was built. Though the South's fall from grace is historical fact, Blanche still argues pointedly, almost a century later, that the decline of culture and gentility holds ramifications far outstepping her personal destiny or that of the society she represents.

Blanche expresses her conviction about the connection between the Stanleys of this world and a generalized devolution of humankind in her lengthy talk to Stella at the close of scene 4. It might be called Blanche's (and Williams's) "what a piece of work is man" speech. In it, she establishes as evidence of humankind's progress toward "being made in God's image" the ideal of "art" ("poetry and music" that help bring "light" out of the chaotic darkness) and "tenderer feelings [that] have had some little beginning." Against this ideal of progress in Blanche's mind stands the reality of Stanley's commonness, his "subhuman," "ape-like," "animal" behavior; he strikes her as a "survivor of the stone age! Bearing the raw meat home from the kill in the jungle!" (83). At this moment Williams employs the sound effect of the passing train (the conventional threat to the helpless maiden in melodrama) to cover Stanley's entrance so he can eavesdrop on his sister-in-law's ringing condemnation of who he is and what he stands for. But the train sound that frames the speech also sets it apart for the audience as no other speech in the play is, indicating the centrality of the statement to the play's meaning. If Blanche's tone at the beginning of the passage seems somewhat hysterical, near the end it becomes more lyrical, but no less urgent in its insistence that Stella not "*hang back with the brutes!*" Instead of evolving toward the godlike, humankind apparently is choosing to regress down the evolutionary ladder toward the animal. In such a world, the powerful are pitted against the defenseless, as described in Williams's poem "Lament for the Moths" from his first collection *In the Winter of Cities* (1956). In the poem, peculiarly appropriate in this context because of Blanche's symbolic association with the moth, the "lovely," "velvety" moths, whose beauty and delicacy had served as a solace to the "troubled" and "neurotic" narrator, are turned to ash by some "pestilent" and "treacherous . . . invisible evil." The concluding stanza takes the form of a prayer that the vulnerable creatures be proffered "strength to enter the heavy world again, / for delicate were the moths and badly wanted / here in a world by mammoth figures haunted!"—this last image an apt symbol for the Stanleys of the world. William Butler Yeats's apocalyptic prophecy in "The Second Coming" of a "rough beast slouching toward Bethlehem" has already come to pass, and it is not just a limited society like Chekhov's Russia at the turn of the century or Williams's South after World War II that is set to experience the loss, but all of civilization that worships the pragmatic and the utilitarian over the less tangible evidence that the human spirit is striving toward transcendence.

"The Histrionic Personality"

In one of the most extensive of his many interviews, Williams specified the source of his identification with Blanche: "We are both hysterics" (*Conversations,* 228). It is not very far into *Streetcar* before his stage directions indicate the particular form her neurosis takes: she delivers her opening line about riding on streetcars called Desire and Cemeteries before alighting at Elysian Fields *"with faintly hysterical humor."* In two articles that appeared in *The American Journal of Psychiatry,* [23] Dr. Paul Chodoff enumerates the behavioral symptoms characteristic of hysteria and defines the sociocultural milieu likely to produce such behavior. These symptoms include flamboyant or histrionic display, hyperemotionality, seductiveness, exhibitionism and sexual maneuvering, linguistic exaggeration, a clinging dependency and demandingness in personal relationships, and a highly developed fantasy life, characterized by the display of a series of "exteriors" as if continually on stage—all of which are visible in Blanche's behavior.

Classically, this neurosis was taken as evidence of a sexual problem, the physical symptoms substituting for repressed and ungratified instincts. Chodoff, however, argues that clinical hysteria "develops under cultural forces of male domination" that prompt a mode of behavior that is actually a travesty or "caricature of femininity." The belittling, male-imposed myth of femininity disallows intellectual curiosity in women in favor of their appearing demure and desirable. A hysteric distorts the traditionally feminine qualities of warmth and expressiveness, and in the most extreme cases, attempts to compensate for her powerlessness by seeking gratification in a series of demeaning and unsatisfactory sexual encounters. (Chodoff finds that the male equivalent of hysteria is macho behavior, a parallel exaggeration of the traditionally masculine characteristics into bellicosity, overcompetitiveness, and vengefulness. Such exaggeration is apparent in Stanley.)

In his director's "Notebook," Kazan proposes that "directing finally consists of turning Psychology into Behavior" (364), which, if *Streetcar* is any indication, is equally true of playwriting as well; Williams has imagined and written the character of Blanche so that her actions reveal her particular neurosis. In her relationship with her younger sister Stella, she is demanding and condescending, treating her almost as a servant. In her general demeanor, she is panicky and overwrought: her speech is feverish; at times she feels faint and exhausted, yet she is full of nervous energy and so must take calming baths; when a cola foams over and stains her white skirt, she cries out in a frenzy as if she herself has been violated—or perhaps in a premonition of what is to come. As Blanche feels more and more trapped by her past guilt and the threat of the present, Williams increases his use of expressionistic techniques—the screeching of the cat, the piano going into a breakdown, the headlights of the locomotive, the Varsouviana and the revolver shot, the lurid reflections and shapes, the sound of inhuman voices, and the repeated echoes—and so reveals her soul state.

Blanche displays the sexually seductive behavior of the histrionic personality by taking a drag on Stanley's cigarette and playfully spraying him with the perfume atomizer, by standing revealed in silk bra and slip in the light and moving suggestively to the music, and by teasing the young paper collector. Her series of one-night liaisons with the young soldiers back in Laurel was a reparation for failing Allan and a surcease from loneliness. But it was also the kind of desperate flailing about for gratification as a compensation for powerlessness that Chodoff identifies. From the moment of her arrival, Blanche feels she must impress Stanley, and her affected and coquettish behavior with Mitch, such as her choice to don the red wrapper for her first moments alone with him, is a capitulation to how society says a woman must act if she is to get a man. The stereotyping by the dominant culture and subsequent caricaturing of certain characteristics as masculine or feminine is another destructive polarity that Williams decries as responsible for modern (wo)man's sense of fragmentation. On the psychological plane, it causes neurotic symptoms such as Blanche's hysteria.

Guilt and Expiation

The most complete statement of Williams's moral system comes through two artist figures, Hannah Jelkes and her grandfather Nonno, in *The Night of the Iguana* (1961). Williams puts forth two chief tenets: as humans, we must accept a fallen world peopled by emotionally and morally frail creatures, and we must reach out to one another with compassion, nonjudgmentally recognizing one another's human weaknesses and responding to each other's needs. Nonno, at ninety-seven the oldest practicing poet in the country (and an affectionate homage to Williams's own grandfather, an Episcopalian priest who lived to a ripe old age), has been working for years on a poem that he finally completes just before his death. The poem is a prayer for courage in the face of imperfection. Nature, like man, lives on after the Fall. Yet nature's ability to rebound with equanimity from the cycle of birth, growth, change, and perpetual decay should fortify man and keep him from despairing at the human condition. The poem emphasizes that to focus on the dark side of existence at the expense of the light is a distortion that leads to inactivity and metaphoric death. This is made personal through the experience of the androgynous and almost ethereal portrait watercolorist Hannah; since she has successfully navigated her own dark night of the soul, she is prepared to help others. She recounts one of the "love" experiences in her life when a terribly lonely man asks if she would remove a piece of her undercloth-ing so he can touch it. Whereas an ordinary individual might recoil from his request and name it dirty, Hannah is moved by his desperate need and complies. She explains her action with the single most forthright statement in the entire Williams canon of how one should measure the morality of an action: "Nothing human disgusts me, unless it is unkind, violent."[24] Her action becomes one of love: altruistically disregarding any inherent tendency to recoil from the man's request, she sees only the depth of his human need.

The word "disgust" links this passage to *Streetcar*, for it was in allowing herself to be prone to such a negative response, however unconsciously and undeliberately, that Blanche failed her young husband in his time of need. Just as Blanche's suitor Mitch has lost someone he found "very sweet" (58), so, too, has Blanche, though she shares a sense of responsibility and so experiences guilt over the loss. As she reveals to Mitch in scene 6, when she was sixteen she fell "much too completely" in love with a young boy—a love that blindingly lit up what before had existed in "shadow." She was attracted to him both because he was "different," with "a softness and tenderness" opposite to the kind of man the cavalier South would favor for a woman, and because of his unarticulated need of her. By the time they returned from their elopement, she knew that she had been unable to answer his unspoken call for "help" and that she had "failed him in some mysterious way." It is only later that she learns, by coming upon him with an older man, of his homosexuality. Pretending nothing had happened and "very drunk," they go out to Moon Lake Casino; while dancing the Varsouviana polka (which she now hears in her mind) and "unable to stop [her]self," she taunted Allan, " 'I saw! I know! You disgust me' " (115). He then ran out and killed himself.

Recognizing her complicity in Allan's death, her violation of Williams's first commandment to accept what is human about the other, her life since then has been a trail of attempted forgetfulness (she reverts to using her maiden name) and of guilt; of sex with, or overtures to, other young men—the soldiers, the seventeen-year-old high school student, the paper boy—to compensate for having rejected Allan, to assuage her guilt, to forestall time; and of drink until she stills the noise of the revolver shot in her head. Having lost her sense of worth and her self-respect, yet needing somehow to counter Allan's death and affirm life through its opposite—desire—she turns with confusion to brief sexual encounters.

The beacon of love that had lighted her world died with Allan, but now Mitch offers the possibility of relighting it. Understanding her need, a need that coincides with her own, he opens his arms to her, and "Sometimes—there's God—so quickly!" (116) He has the ability to quiet Blanche's guilt and restore her self-respect, but only by unquestioningly accepting her for what she is—an emotionally distraught yet spiritually valuable person. He has the opportunity to do for Blanche what she was unable to do for Allan, perhaps through her own inadequacy and frustration. Finally, though, Mitch is not up to the task. He cannot go beyond the ethical categories that society imposes and by which society judges, and thus forgive rather than condemn her. Her dual punishments are rejection by Mitch (and to a lesser extent, by Stella) and Stanley's rape. The ceremony at which Blanche is the sacrificial victim takes on the aura of a desecrated marriage; even the gown is dulled by time. Though Stanley wears silk wedding pajamas, he is not her bridegroom, nor will she ever now experience a life-giving consummation. Although some commentators have seen Blanche as masochistically desiring the violation, suffering from a death wish, Williams's stage directions reject any conscious submission on her part: "*She cries out and strikes at him with the bottle top but he catches her wrist. She moans. The bottle top falls. She sinks to her knees. He picks up her inert figure and carries her to the bed*" (162).

Williams indicates, through the convergence of clothing imagery and religious symbology in *Streetcar's* closing scene, that the psychic and physical violence done to Blanche atones her guilt and reasserts her gallantry. Early in scene 2 when Stanley catalogues Blanche's possessions, Stella corrects his appraisal of her wardrobe, thus undercutting appearance by reality: the "genuine fox-fur pieces" are only "inexpensive summer" ones, the "crown for an empress" only "a rhinestone tiara she wore to a costume ball" (34–35). By scene 10, Blanche herself accepts the fact that exteriors, the "transitory possession[s]," can no longer mask the truth and are never of any value unless they image forth an interior reality. At the end of the play, Williams appropriately employs clothing to mirror the spiritual transformation his heroine has undergone. Blanche emerges radiant from the last of her ritual expiatory baths clothed in a "Della Robbia blue [jacket], the blue of the robe in the old Madonna pictures"; she hears the ringing of the "clean" cathedral bells and fingers "*the bunch of grapes which Eunice had brought in*" (169). Grapes are the source of the wine that becomes Christ's cleansing blood during the Eucharist and that iconographically suggest wisdom in Renaissance paintings of the Madonna and Child. Blanche leaves the stage a violated Madonna, blessed by whatever saving grace insanity/illusion can provide. The closed world of her mind (madness tempering pain) is analogous to the artificial world of the theater (magic offsetting reality) that the audience temporarily inhabits. Art and imagination become a kind of sacrament, not only in the scheme of Blanche's redemption but for the audience as well: art makes the word flesh so that the audience can bear such pain and perhaps even experience an epiphany.

The Question of Tragedy

For centuries, critics and theorists from Aristotle in the classical period through Friedrich Nietzsche in the nineteenth century and George Steiner in the twentieth have been defining and debating the nature of tragic drama, but especially in the late 1940s and early 1950s this became a popular subject for discussion among American theatergoers as well. One impetus was Arthur Miller's essay "Tragedy and the Common Man" (1949), which was inspired in part by the response of reviewers and audiences to his recent *Death of a Salesman*. According to Miller's formulation, any person acting in a fully human fashion, regardless of his or her position on the social scale, is a fit subject for tragedy if he or she would willingly "lay down . . . life" itself "to secure . . . [a] sense of personal dignity." Miller turned on its head Aristotle's notion that the tragic hero is inherently flawed by some error in judgment that brings about a downfall. No longer was the notion of a "flaw" encumbered by negative connotations: to be flawed, to refuse to "remain passive in the face of what he conceives to be a challenge to his dignity, his image of his rightful status,"[25] becomes the very source of the tragic figure's integrity. This is humankind's potential and, finally, its glory.

Even *Life* magazine entered this renewed cultural debate. An editorial entitled "Untragic America" reminded readers that one of the signs of the "great civilizations" of the past—Athens during the fourth century B.C. or the England of Shakespeare's time—was the flowering of tragic drama. The editorial worried openly (perhaps in a veiled reflection on the aftermath of the dropping of the atom bomb) that our loss of a "sense of sin" and of "man's cosmic importance" caused a lack of tragic drama in America. This weakness in the fabric of society can only be repaired if man, though capable of rising to greatness, once again recognizes that overreaching his "finiteness" may result in bringing punishment down upon himself.

Almost from inception, *A Streetcar Named Desire* has been recurrently linked by its creators and critics with the word "tragedy." Remarking on its thematic emphasis, the playwright referred to *Streetcar* as a "tragedy of incomprehension" (*Essays*, 109); attempting to categorize its theatrical style in his production diary, Kazan, the director of the original production, termed Streetcar "a poetic tragedy," revealing "the death of something extraordinary . . . the final dissolution of a person of worth, who once had great potential, and who, even as she goes down, has worth exceeding that of the 'healthy,' coarse-grained figures who kill her" ("Notebook," 365). Phrases such as "almost unbearably tragic," "tragic overtones of grand opera," "somber tragedy," "abiding tragedy," "true tragedy," and "a savagely arresting tragedy [that lacks the] nobility of high tragedy" all appear in the initial reviews without much attempt to demonstrate the appropriateness of the designation.[26] Yet even among scholars definitions of tragedy are more various and less rigidly applied than they once were. If the audience usually measures the tragic experience by the emotional and intellectual impact of the work, critics are more likely to attend to the question of the protagonist's responsibility and self-recognition: the hero's suffering must not seem totally gratuitous, but should be invested with a sense of rightness or universal sanction and should lead to illumination rather than senseless pain.

Early character analyses of Blanche first raised the central issue of her options and choices, of her power to control her own fate: Is her defeat, as Robert Emmet Jones suggests, inevitable because she is passive in the face of "social forces" and fails to "battle her destiny," and thus becomes merely "pathetic and melodramatic"?[27] Or, as the Marxist critic Harry Taylor argues, is Blanche from the very beginning too "hazy-minded" and lacking in will to win the conflict rather than simply endure a series of confrontations with a "monstrously destructive and implacable" convergence of forces?[28] Because the performance time is necessarily limited, the dramatic form is able to delineate the causal relationship between actions and their consequences particularly well. From this perspective, Williams perhaps fails in not allowing Blanche (whose grip on reality is faltering anyway)—and even more so the audience—to comprehend any connection between her betrayal of Allan and her final violation at the hands of Stanley that would make it something other than simply a random act of brutality.

Certainly Williams has given Blanche character flaws aplenty: her carnality and exhibitionism, her vanity and posturing, her duplicity, deceitfulness and slender grasp on reality, her selfishness, condescension and self-pity. Her hubris reveals itself in characteristics that are ambiguous in the best sense of the word: her belief in her own specialness, her perceived excess of imagination that simultaneously alienates her from others yet serves as a source of her salvation, and her ill-fated attempt to deny the material in favor of the spiritual, rather than attain transcendence *through* matter as all humankind must. Yet these flaws are balanced by what Jessica Tandy, who originated the role of Blanche on stage, saw as her "pathetic elegance," "indomitable spirit" and "innate tenderness" (Letter, 105). Despite the audience's uneasiness over whether Blanche's retreat into the saving world of illusion can totally succeed, the serenity that comes after the catastrophe invests her with a "gallantry" in defeat and a tragic grandeur. Williams's notion of tragedy might be most similar to that of the novelist Edith Wharton (as once delineated by Alfred Kazin): "the failure of love and personal isolation."[29] And whether in the end one sees *Streetcar* as tragic and Blanche as a tragic heroine who consciously undergoes a purgation and experiences a regeneration, or simply as a pathological victim, more sinned against than sinning, the final effect of this play does not change: it is still, regardless of categorization invited or imposed, the same rich and moving theatrical and literary experience.

If Williams leaves open the question of Blanche's tragic nature, he is more emphatic that *Streetcar* is about the tragedy of modern civilization. The materialistic, mechanistic, utilitarian world of the audience sees beauty, sensitivity, and sensibility as expendable and threatening to its way of life; it does not want to ask the aesthetic and moral questions that the Blanches of this world demand; and it insists on destroying what it does not want and cannot have. This throws onto the audience, rather than the protagonist, the burden of enlightenment that is a necessary outcome of the tragic experience. The spectator leaves unsettled and disquieted, in contrast to Blanche's seeming calm and possible portion of grace at the end of the play. The play and the protagonist are finally cut of the same cloth: *Streetcar* is gutsy, yet exquisitely sensitive, both mothlike in its lyricism and powerful in its earthiness, boldly imaginative in its flights into magic yet grounded in a recognition of what is human in all of us. To respond empathetically to Blanche is to accept the beauty of the play which is also hers, and vice versa.

7

Stanley

The Ideology of Domination

If Blanche costumed in her ball gown and tiara is a princess from the faded past, Stanley in his colorful raiment acts as "king" of his limited domain—a run-down apartment in the French Quarter. His wife, Stella, and his buddies from work are his loyal subjects. That Stanley can look upon Blanche's arrival as an invasion and threat to the absolute control he exercises over his territory intimates the precariousness of his position. Vulnerable to criticism for his rough and uncultivated behavior, he is threatened by Blanche's pretensions to refinement and gentility. Blanche can remind his wife of what she sacrificed to marry him and of the severe limitations on what he has been able to provide her in return. His power and his pride as a man rest in his virility: he is the "gaudy seed-bearer" whose be-all and end-all is the "giving and taking" (25) of physical pleasure.

Stanley apparently seemed to promise Stella something more. A decorated master sergeant in the Engineers Corps during the war but now on the road for a company where the men who hang out with him also work, Stanley is the only one of his crowd, Stella believes, who will "get anywhere" (52), though she has little evidence except for his "drive." The prosperity of the post-World War II years has eluded him and disillusionment with his lot and with a system that does not guarantee personal success even to those who fought to protect it has set in. Stanley is insecure about his potential to be or do anything other than what he is and does. As a later American playwright Sam Shepard says about these returning World War II veterans, " 'You get the sense that they had their "day," and their day is now passed, but there's not much for 'em to look forward to.' "[30] Since Stanley has been unable, except in bed, to make Stella his queen, even Blanche's cheap imitation furs and jewelry are indictments that only exacerbate his insecurity. If Stella and Blanche's "improvident" ancestors lived by their libidos, so too does Stanley, whose animal force can only be accommodated in the sexual act. That their ancestors finally lost Belle Reve through their uncontrolled libido, their "epic fornications," points to the ultimate deficiency of this ethic. Stanley does not bother to think in moral terms: all is right with the world if "the colored lights" between himself and Stella are going once again, as they will be when Blanche is exiled.

In his recent book *The Betrayal of the Self: The Fear of Autonomy in Men and Women* (1988), the psychotherapist Arno Gruen puts forth a theory about human developmᵊnt that helps explain Stanley's personality. According to Gruen, most nᵊn live in fear of facing their vulnerability because it cannot be integrated with their own abstract notion of themselves as strong, decisive, and powerful—a self-image that repeatedly needs confirmation through the "admiration" offered by women. Consequently, they shy away from expressing "suffering and helplessness as signs of weakness," which threaten to become self-fulfilling prophecies. Instead they choose to oppress and dominate, exerting "power and control as means of denying helplessness." But to do this, to hold in contempt any stirrings of "sorrow and pain, to deride openness and flexibility, [women's] creative potential, vitality and tenderness is to destroy one's own autonomy." Developing and affirming one's sense of autonomy, on the other hand, "entails having a self with access to its own feelings and needs." When men betray the self by choosing the ideology of power in preference to the way of love, women are forced to become "divided" selves, to suppress "their most profound experiences [which] contradict official reality" as defined by men. The need for others to strengthen us in our delusions becomes, finally, a "source of human self-destructiveness and evil."[31]

Since Stanley can not control through moral force, he exerts his authority through purely physical means. When made ashamed of his limitations of class and sensibility, he retaliates. He is a smasher, not only of objects but of people; he becomes increasingly violent as the play proceeds. He is a stalker, foxlike in his stealth, who rules his territory by destructively preying upon others. Swinish in his manners, he tosses watermelon rinds on the floor and throws dishes from the table when told he eats like a pig and should help clean his own place. Just as he triumphantly smashed all the light bulbs on his wedding night, he now slams drawers and throws a radio out the window to demonstrate he is boss. He violates Blanche's possessions—her trunk, her clothes and jewelry, the love letters from her dead husband, the paper lantern—until he finally becomes her "executioner." After buying her a return ticket to Laurel as a birthday present and cruelly destroying her only hope for the future by telling Mitch of her past, he rapes Blanche. During the rape, through the transparent back wall of the apartment, the audience sees a streetwalker being pursued by a drunk she has rolled; she, in turn, loses her "sequined bag" to a thief. For having threatened Stanley's little domain, Blanche becomes another object to be used and discarded; Stanley reasserts his vengeful supremacy through brute strength. In his rage and self-disgust, he is to Blanche as she was to Allan, but with a central distinction: whereas Blanche's cruelty was unthinking and, therefore, forgivable, Stanley's is malevolent, and therefore not.

All value, to Stanley, must be measurable to the senses and capable of being possessed or controlled physically. Generally, Williams decries facticity, valorizing imaginative insight and revelation over "empiric evidence" (*Essays*, 55). A literalist or anti-illusionist, Stanley names Blanche's fantasies all lies and deceits, unable to see any aesthetic or potentially redemptive value in the "magic" she creates. If props contribute to Blanche's power as an illusionist, for Stanley possessions are proof only of *being* someone. Not that Stanley is without his theatrical side: he changes costume (from denim work clothes to silk bowling shirt to silk pajamas) frequently and sometimes exhibitionistically; he depends on broad gestures, on swaggering and strutting, to impress. He also fosters the illusion—more destructive than any of Blanche's—that he did not assault his sister-in-law, a lie that ultimately destroys her as well as Mitch, and that fractures with doubt his relationship with Stella.

Totally pragmatic, he demands that a woman "lay her cards on the table" and measures her worth by how readily she does so. Seemingly without sentiment in his relationship with others, he cannot understand why Blanche values the yellowing love letters from a dead boy, since they have no measurable worth in the present. And yet Stanley must harbor a few hints of softness and sensitivity to make Stella's physical attraction and worship of him credible. Stella must be responding to something beyond her own need to run from death to life through sensual fulfillment. So if there exists a Stanley-side to Blanche's character, as her red satin robe suggests, there also seems to be a Blanche-side to Stanley. Stanley's sobs of anguish over the fear that Stella has left are inklings of a softer element, though they may only show he is aware of just how precarious his hold on her is.

Text versus Performance

By controlling the audience response of identification and empathy, an actor can radically effect, even alter, the interpretation of a play. More than most modern dramatic texts—and due in part to the very richness of its characterizations along with split sympathies for *both* Blanche and Stanley that its author confesses to in extratextual remarks (*Conversations*, 277)—*A Streetcar Named Desire* is open and available to a directorial emphasis which, though it may not distort the play completely, might seem to run counter to the author's intention, as expressed in verbal and visual codes in the text. In the original production of *Streetcar,* this apparently occurred with Marlon Brando's portrayal of Stanley Kowalski—one of the most famous renditions ever by an American actor in any role, and one which solidified the primacy of the method of the Actors Studio, where Brando received his training, for a whole generation of young actors and actresses (including such stars as Paul Newman and Geraldine Page who later appeared together in Williams's *Sweet Bird of Youth*).

Williams's text makes it clear that abusiveness coexists with some tenderness in Stanley's personality. Yet according to Eric Bentley, the performance by Brando, to whom "brutishness [is] not native," heightened the tender undercurrents in the role, with the result that "tough talk . . . mask[ed] a suffering sensitive soul."[32] Although Stanley shows he is vulnerable through the tenuousness of his hold on Stella, the text does not sanction interpreting Stanley as either someone who possesses so many tender emotions, over which he feels shame and embarrassment, that he must hide them through outward assertiveness and bravado, or as someone whose aggressive masculinity is a mask for the fear of the feminine in his own nature. Still, Williams apparently sensed and responded to that feminine sensitivity beneath the surface in Brando when determining his rightness for the part. The initial production apparently allowed the personality of the performer to tip the balance in favor of Stanley's tenderness over his violence (at least for a considerable portion of the play) with a concomitant shift in audience sympathy.

Something else was also at work in the actor/spectator dynamic which came to disturb Jessica Tandy, the actress playing Blanche. In a letter to Williams in which she refused to pose for a promotional photo of Blanche provocatively clad in a silk slip, she expressed fear that the audience wanted a "sexy, salacious play." She also understood that it is easier for an audience to identify with Stanley's "unadulterated guts" than with Blanche's refined, if overwrought, sensibilities (Letter, 105). Stanley does, indeed, conform to society's stereotypical notions of what is normal and healthy: the sexuality of his marriage, however aggressive, is natural and without guilt; his reaction to Blanche's pretensions and condescension, however retaliatory, is an assertion of the dignity of the blue-collar class that refuses to be ashamed of its social position. Furthermore, he displays a humor that, however crude and vulgar, aids his survival, much as Blanche's fantasies do hers. Finally, perhaps the audience's very sense of Stanley's powerlessness to "make it" in the "rat race" influences them to applaud his competitiveness and aggressiveness that refuses to lie down in defeat. When a mass audience shares that sense of powerlessness and broken promises as they did in the late 1940s, or when they believe advance in the business world comes more quickly when ethical concerns can be ignored as happened in the late 1980s, the more strongly they will be tempted to assent to and applaud Stanley's actions.

The Lawrentian Matrix

In *Streetcar,* an insistent pattern of dichotomous images proclaims the fragmentation between masculine and feminine in modern life—and the absence of a much-needed integrative principle. How closely does Stanley and Stella's marriage approach an ideal balance between the masculine and feminine sensibilities, between an earthy instinctual response to life and an intellectual, ethical one, between lust and love? On examination, their marriage has not fulfilled its initial promise as a Lawrentian communion in which pagan naturalism attains religious value. In D. H. Lawrence, whose influence Williams often acknowledges, physical sexuality, as Marion Magid reminds us (in "The Innocence of Tennessee Williams," *Commentary,* January 1963), undergoes a deification and thus serves as a civilizing or humanizing force for humankind. Transcendence comes in and through the physical, which is never denied or left behind, only sanctified. Yet, for the phallocentric Stanley, his union with Stella is a hedonistic counter to his own inner frustrations, rooted in momentary pleasure and release, and partaking not at all of the sacramental. He has not the least qualm about betraying Stella on the very night that the symbol of their generative bond, the child, is born. Stanley's crudeness reveals that his lust has not been purified and transformed into love.

Stanley

Stanley's actions in violating Blanche and, at the same time, his marriage vows with Stella are life-denying rather than life-generating. A marriage union that had been joyful and sacred for Stella in its sexuality is so in the end only as the source of the child that brings to fruition her deep maternal needs. Although Williams later situates the play's meaning in the fact that Stanley "does go on with her" (*Conversations*, 275), Stanley does so solely at the level of animality or carnality. With time comes the possibility that Stella will turn more and more away from the husband and toward the child to fulfill her emotional needs.

Rituals of Machoism

Williams incorporates a number of rituals into *A Streetcar Named Desire*. Some have Blanche as their center: her recurrent hot baths which serve as rites of purification; and her aborted birthday party, where the uneaten cake not only symbolizes her refusal to accept time's passing but, with Mitch's absence, foreshadows their final breakup—a rite of failed communion. Still others, such as the poker parties and the (off-stage) bowling, center on Stanley (and his friends). Williams even designates scene 3 as "The Poker Night," which was one of the titles he had earlier considered for the entire work. (It is also the title of a now-famous Thomas Hart Benton painting illustrating scene 3 that the producer, Irene Mayer Selznick, presented to the playwright.) His stage description for that scene, specifying *"raw"* primary colors (*"yellow linoleum," "vivid green glass shade"* over the light, and *"vivid slices of watermelon"*) mentions *"a picture of Van Gogh's of a billiard-parlor at night"* (46). In an article that identifies the painting as van Gogh's *All Night Cafe*, Henry Schvey describes the expressionistic canvas as "marked by the contrasts of blood red walls and yellow floor with a dark green, coffin-shaped billiard table set diagonally in the middle, casting an ominous shadow," and then quotes from a letter by van Gogh in which the painter designates " 'the cafe [as] a place where one can ruin oneself, go mad, or commit a crime.' "³³

Peopling this scene are Stanley and his drinking buddies clothed in brightly colored shirts (*"solid blues, a purple, a red-and-white check, a light green"*) and *"at the peak of their physical manhood, as coarse and direct as the primary colors"* (49). Williams's description hearkens back to Stanley's first appearance in the play. With its crude if hearty humor, its unmannerly eating and drinking, and its eruptions into challenges and caustic remarks, the game, like most locker-room assertions of masculinity, offers these men both a moment of bonding in which they can sublimate their otherwise unmet emotional needs and also a proof of their manliness: competition, aggressiveness, and finally domination are the rules. The game, in session once again at the end of the play, provides the play's closing line: "This game is seven-card stud" (179). The rules of Stanley's game ultimately triumph over the rubrics of Blanche's rituals. Yet another ritual suggests a kind of perverse baptismal rite. Stanley's celebratory and phallic squirting of the foaming beer over his head at the beginning of scene 10 not only recalls Blanche's hysterical premonitory outburst when the foaming Coke spotted her virginal white skirt but also visually presages the rape to come. The generative sexuality that resulted in the birth of the child is thus contrasted with the purely abusive attack on Blanche that is destructive rather than procreative.

Through these rituals, Williams paints a picture of what might be termed "The New Man," whom he decries. There exists deliberate ambiguity in Stanley's personality—a healthy normalcy about the physical and a vulnerability submerged beneath the macho front American society demands of its men. Still, his crudeness, commonness, and lack of moral discrimination finally render him animal-like in more than just his stealth and grease-stained look, and culminate in Stanley as rapist and violator. If Blanche turns to art and the imagination as a compensation for her incompleteness, Stanley turns to violence. For the Stanleys to take over the world would mean a universal coarsening and diminishment. Stanley is like Caliban in Shakespeare's *The Tempest:* he would destroy the books—the civilizing agents—in Prospero's library.

Stanley

In the antinomies around which Williams structures his play, he evidences the culturally conditioned tendency to designate certain qualities as masculine and others as feminine. But the play itself works against perpetuating these ultimately destructive stereotypes. Particularly through Blanche, who is both attracted to and repelled by a confidence and strength she sees in Stanley yet knows that she can never attain (he has no "nervous bone[s] in his body" [79]), Williams indicates that incompleteness results when men and women are forced into restricted modes of thinking and action, rather than permitted to integrate within one personality both tenderness *and* strength. Yet even if Stanley is a victim of society's definition of maleness which makes him submerge and deny his affective side, his treatment of Blanche is still abusive and capricious in the extreme. Frightened over the tenuousness of his relationship with Stella, he lashes out at Blanche as the nearest object of his wrath.

8

Stella

"Stella for Star"

When Blanche and Mitch return, at the beginning of scene 6, to the Kowalskis' flat in the Quarter after their lackluster night at the amusement park on Lake Pontchartrain, Blanche glances into the sky to look at the constellation of the Pleiades, the seven mythological sisters who took refuge from the amorous pursuit of Orion by fleeing into the realm of the eternal. Earlier that same evening, when the Young Man came knocking at the Kowalskis' door at the close of scene 5 "collecting for *The Evening Star*," Blanche's fey attempt at a humorous rejoinder, "I didn't know that stars took up collections" (96), hints at the disjunction between the heavenly and the material. Near the opening of scene 1, Blanche's words of greeting to her sister end with a frenzied "Stella for Star!" (10). This sister "star" has, at least from one perspective, plummeted from the ethereal to the earthly: her source of transcendence is no longer found in the "beautiful dream" of a pillared plantation but in the phenomenon of "colored lights" ignited metaphorically in the here-and-now by a husband's ardor. Leaving Blanche to deal alone with the dying, Stella had escaped ten years previously from the ancestral homestead which was left, after the death of their father, without a male protector. She returned only for the funerals of the remaining female relatives, and was finally romantically swept off her feet by her much "decorated" army officer. If the overbearing Blanche, who continues to refer to Stella as "baby," both fawned over and made demands on her younger sister, she did little to prevent Stella from seeking out a marriage of dependency and even docility, yet one that would also release her sexuality and fulfill her maternal longings. Blanche is still fighting for possession of Stella, hoping that her sister will sanction her value system and reconfirm allegiance to her and her way of life over Stanley's.

Having traded the desiccation and spiritual decay of Belle Reve for the vibrancy and physical vitality of the French Quarter, Stella has made a healthy adjustment that delivers her from Blanche's neuroticism. Accepting the physical as a necessary component of the spiritual and desire as normal has liberated her—though perhaps only for another kind of enslavement. For, when Blanche intrudes upon the Kowalski household, she finds a Stella in early pregnancy who defines herself almost totally in terms of Stanley. A captive worshipper at the altar of her husband, the "luxurious" Stella, now *"serene"* with a look of *"almost narcotized tranquility"* (70), has given up classical culture for comic books and traded genteel manners for the thrill of seeing Stanley smash all the light bulbs on their wedding night. His world and friends define the parameters of her own, and a week's physical separation makes her go "wild." She and the other women in their crowd, despite occasional grumblings and defensive outbursts, have few inner resources of their own. They are content to live in a world defined by males and their social rituals, to be called "the little woman" and to trot along behind the men and watch them bowl, to countenance, up to a point, their card playing and loud drinking because of what will happen later in the bedroom. Even verbal and physical abuse do not keep Stella away from Stanley for long: near the end of scene 3, faced with Blanche's abhorrence over what she is about to do, Stella defies her sister, goes down the stairs, and surrenders herself to the same man who only moments before had physically abused her. Several times in

Streetcar, Stella, denying that her condition is in any way "desperate" or that she lives in a situation that she wants "to get out of," is positioned to choose between Blanche and Stanley. The choice, up until the final moments of the play, almost invariably falls to husband over sister.

Williams demarcates the subtle shift in Stanley and Stella's relationship through a carefully placed series of visual images, such as late in scene 3, in which the wife either actively responds to her husband's entreaties or withholds herself from him. In response to Stanley's mournful pleas that his "baby doll" come back to him, Stella descends the stairs in her blue satin kimono to meet his "animal moans" with her own. Totally at her mercy, he kneels and puts his face against her pregnant belly and then carries her into their bedroom. (This image of Stanley *"lift[ing] her off her feet and bear[ing] her into the dark flat"* [67] is ominously recalled when Stanley *"picks up [Blanche's] inert figure and carries her to the bed"* [162] during the rape.) Early in the play, the unborn child is still unitive and not disruptive of Stanley and Stella's relationship. Only at the end of scene 8, when Stella goes into labor, will Stanley again treat his wife with such tender solicitude. Earlier, at the close of scene 4, after reluctantly hearing Blanche's tirade against Stanley's commonness and her admonition not to *"hang back with the brutes!"* (83) Stella—perhaps sensing the truth in Blanche's assessment—*"fiercely"* embraces the grease-stained Stanley as he grins triumphantly at Blanche. But in scene 7, Stella withdraws from her husband's embrace, albeit only *"gently,"* after Stanley's rendition of Blanche's past, which she accepts as *"partly"* the truth but then attempts to rationalize away.

The Broken Family

The final image in this pattern occurs at the very close of the play after Blanche's departure on the arm of the Doctor, and brings into question the nature of any continuing relationship between Stanley and Stella. Any doubts about Stella's absolute commitment to Stanley stirred up by Blanche's set piece about "the brutes" or by her sacrifice of "tenderer feelings" to keep her marriage vital, have solidified. Her plaintive lament, "Oh, God, what have I done to my sister?" (176), reveals her growing realization and the depth of her guilt over not believing in Blanche's goodness and in her accusations against Stanley. Initially, she justified her acceptance of Stanley's lie over Blanche's elemental truth with the rationalization, "I couldn't believe her story and go on living with Stanley" (165). Yet her awareness of the Matron's potential cruelty and her fear of the "hurt" that may be inflicted on her sister at the asylum leave Stella forever in doubt about her husband: things can never be the same between them again. The possibility that Blanche the fabulist may indeed be the truth teller, and that Stanley the empiricist may not be above distorting the facts when it suits his purpose, will continue to gnaw at Stella. When Eunice places the male child swaddled *"in a pale blue blanket"* (178) in Stella's arms, the visual stage icon is momentarily that of the Madonna and Child. Yet Stanley's lustful action as he once again *"kneels"* (as in scene 3) and moves *"his fingers [to] find the opening of her blouse"* (179) belies any notion that this is a holy family bonded in selfless love. If Blanche was an intruder who threatened their relationship, now the baby intrudes between Stanley and Stella. In forcing Blanche's expulsion, Stanley has, ironically, driven a wedge between himself and Stella, further fracturing the relationship he had hoped to protect.

Stanley never indicates that the child signifies anything more to him than his own potency. He celebrates the announcement of his son's arrival—born the night he betrays his union with Stella by violating Blanche—by waving, as a banner of his virility, the red silk pajamas he had worn on his wedding night. Neither the child nor its mother is in his thoughts at play's end—only once again getting "the colored lights going with nobody's sister behind the curtain to hear us!" (133). Stella's lack of response to Stanley's groping and *"sensual murmur[ing]"* as she continues the *"luxurious"* sobbing over her share in Blanche's destruction suggest that the child will now become the center of her being, the focus of her attention and love as the nurturing mother takes preeminence over the wife and lover. Her decisive turn *"inward as if some interior voice had called her name"* (137) at the moment she went into labor signals a permanent shift in alignment. While Stella may be there *for* Stanley's use as a sex object in the future, she indicates she will never again be totally *with* him as energetic lover.

The Upstairs Neighbors

The baby is born on Blanche's birthday, after the abortive party and during the rape that seals her fate, suggesting the child is linked to her as well. He is the child whom she never had (she wants Stella to save the birthday candles to use someday for the baby's cake), but also the male offspring who will rejuvenate her family's blood by "mixing" it with the healthy Stanley's. Williams ensures, however, that the audience does not sentimentalize the generative sexuality of Stanley and Stella's marriage nor ignore the deficiencies of a union centered purely on the physical through the presence of the Hubbels, the Kowalskis' upstairs neighbors. Their raucous behavior provides a parodistic exaggeration of a meeting of bodies devoid of soul. Steve and Eunice's earthy love/hate relationship, though one-dimensional as befits a subsidiary plot, differs from Stanley and Stella's not in its essential nature, but only in degree.

Steve's animal noises, his "goat-like screeches" and "bellowing laughter," his raunchy story of the rooster chasing the hen, and his eruptions into noise and physical violence all link him with Stanley. And Steve and Eunice's relationship exhibits the same abrupt and barely controlled shifts from noisy arguments to moments of intense physical affection that characterize Stanley and Stella's attraction toward one another. Eunice even parallels Stella in the way she enthusiastically welcomes Steve back after one of his outbursts solely for the physical pleasure he can provide. Williams gives Steve the unalterably harsh curtain line, "This game is seven-card stud," making him an emphatic choral messenger of the new brutal ways that have displaced Blanche's attempts to assure the continuance of the civilized—and civilizing—arts and emotions. And, in the final scene as well, Williams has Eunice counsel Stella in the pragmatic, "life-has-got-to-go-on" ethic that valorizes continued sexual fulfillment over a morally assertive and positive response to Blanche's desperate cry for help. Stella becomes one more (like Blanche with Allan, and Mitch with Blanche) who has either not been willing or able to risk self to respond to another in time of need.

The Strindbergian Matrix

The presence of Steve and Eunice in the play helps to place in doubt— as does the absence of any civilizing side to Stanley's exuberant animality—the legitimacy of considering D. H. Lawrence's vision of sexual union as an appropriate analogue for Stanley and Stella. Rather than discover in the play a Lawrentian aura of exalted pagan sexuality, a more telling frame of reference is August Strindberg. *A Streetcar Named Desire* not only reflects the eternal battle of the sexes between the archetypal male and female principles, but also reflects the Scandinavian dramatist's imagery. Strindberg writes of being brought down from the heights, both social and moral, to the depths, from the ethereal into the mud and muck, which suggests the notion of a progressive fall from an Edenic past.

Stella's literal action of descending the stairs in scene 3, of willingly coming down to Stanley's level, is a dramatic visualization of Stanley's taunting reminder in scene 8 that she chose to marry him even though he "was common as dirt": he pulled her "down off them columns and how [she] loved it, having them colored lights going!" (137). As in Strindberg's *Miss Julie* (1888), one of the last remnants of the old aristocracy succumbs to the rising business class. This comparison casts a peculiar light on *Streetcar* as social drama, since Stanley, the agent of democratization who would be inherently attractive to a middle-class audience (no matter how intellectually highbrow) is deficient in all values except physical strength. Williams suggests this is the price society must pay for rejecting aristocratic values that might betray the least trace of elitism in its attempt to approach egalitarianism.

But vitality without moral, ethical, or aesthetic values is a poor replacement for even a weakened gentility. True to Strindberg's pattern, the union between Stanley and Stella is not a communion but a meeting that can only exist between a victor and a defeated one. Although Williams would later remark somewhat cryptically that "the meaning of the play is that [Stanley] does go on with [Stella]" (*Conversations*, 275), whether or not Stanley is victorious in imposing upon Stella an identity that defines her by submission remains satisfyingly ambiguous as the curtain falls.

9

Mitch

"How do I love thee?"

The guilt that Stella feels at play's end over turning her back on Blanche—choosing for her own and her child's preservation Stanley's base lie over her sister's truth—is shared by Mitch, who fails Blanche in much the same way as she earlier had failed her young husband. Blanche's responsibility lay not in her inability to change Allan Grey's personality, no matter how much he himself might have hoped for that when he cried out to her for help; rather, it resides in her "disgust," her judgmental condemnation of his homosexuality that destroys his already shakey sense of self-worth and drives him to suicide. Mitch, too, proves unable to accept Blanche for what she has been in the past and is in the present, and thus helps rob her of whatever dignity and grace she can still summon forth. Yet if Blanche was doomed to fail in her efforts to save Allan, Williams indicates that Mitch might have made a difference for Blanche—and she for him. In their mutual acceptance of one another, they might have acted as a God, as a compassionate forgiving savior for the other. But Mitch's belated gestures toward the end of scene 11, his sagging energy, distracted gaze, and then his

67

ineffectual attempt to push Stanley out of the way and go gallantly to Blanche's rescue, are too little too late. He is left as the curtain falls with tears over what has happened, not only to Blanche but to himself, and over the part he has played in it.

Just as Blanche lost the young poet she loved "unendurably," so has there been a loss in Mitch's past. "A very strange, very sweet" dying girl left him a silver cigarette case inscribed with the final lines of what coincidentally happens to be Blanche's "favorite sonnet" by Elizabeth Barrett Browning: "And if God choose, / I shall but love thee better after death." The poem intimates there need be no disjunction between love and death, that death does not end a complete and total love, but only perfects it. The love in the poem, never much grounded in the physical, sought a retreat to a condition of innocence and unquestioning devotion. This ended abruptly, coinciding with the demise of the persona's religious faith in her other "lost saints." Yet for Williams, idealized love is unlikely to be tolerant of human needs, the loneliness and failures that make the loved one most desperate for—and most deserving of—someone reaching out to bring surcease from hurt. And so the quotation from Browning cuts two ways: in the hereafter, love might overcome death; for Williams, however, to fail to love realistically—if imperfectly—in the present, on whatever level the loved one requires to be made whole, is loss. This loss results in the guilt and remorse that Blanche feels, and that Stella and Mitch also experience.

Blanche's Gentleman Caller

When Blanche first sees Mitch at the poker night, she immediately notices a "sort of sensitive look" that she hardly expects to find among Stanley's crowd and that makes him appear somehow "superior to the others" (52). The dying girl must have sensed this quality as well; it perhaps also echoes the sensitivity that characterized and finally consumed Allan. If the somewhat beefy, heavyset, and ungraceful Mitch is physically not at all like Blanche's young husband, there is an analogously disquieting side to him psychologically. Except for an inordinate attachment to his dying mother, he has not had a sustained relationship. Although protesting his intense love for his mother, he also deeply resents the possessiveness and jealousy that inhibit him and restrict his choices. Mitch is something of a misfit among Stanley's friends: he is older, without a woman, and though only halfheartedly interested in drinking and card playing, participates because it makes him part of the group. Mitch also suffers the men's ribbing for not being able to host a game at his ailing mother's house and for having to go home early to check on her. His exclusive attachment to her needs at the expense of a mature relationship of his own threatens to leave him lonely when she dies; she will, in effect, continue to control him after her death.

Brought up to be a gentleman, Mitch is emotionally clumsy and fumbling in his interactions with Blanche, which is what one side of her demands. Yet he is also full of pent-up sexuality that leaves him prey to Blanche's allure. His excessive gallantry, nurtured in a matriarchal household, mixes uneasily with his barely controlled sexual urges. His good manners are also a pose that Blanche demands he exhibit, as when at the close of scene 5 he must "bow" and play her "Rosenkavalier." Mitch needs Blanche's tenderness to help him break free of his mother and belatedly complete a process of individuation and maturation that has been denied him. Despite her own vulnerability, Blanche can potentially do as much for Mitch as he can for her. When in scene 9, after discovering Blanche's past, he rejects any possibility of marriage since she is "not clean enough to bring in the house with [his] mother" (150), Mitch chooses to continue in his past dependency rather than risk full self-realization. On another level, he judges and finds Blanche wanting by the very same code of conventional moral behavior that, ironically, she pretends to uphold and demands that he adhere to. What dominates his motives is his fear of sullying what has been the deepest—and ultimately the most debilitating—emotional attachment of his life, that of son to emasculating mother.

The Stanley in Mitch

Mitch considers the unvirginal Blanche unfit as a wife to be taken home to his mother; he comes eventually to treat her as a whore, to reduce her humanity as others before him have done and as Stanley soon will. Not only in the volatility and barely controlled violence of a man unable to control his own life, but also in his reliance on discovering "the facts" about Blanche's past escapades instead of listening to what his heart and his instincts tell him, Mitch resembles Stanley. Just as Stanley boasts about how he will uncover the truth about Blanche, Mitch seeks out the same evidence. Like a similarly misguided Othello, who also sought experiential proof, Mitch places phone calls to Blanche's home town of Laurel to verify the stories Stanley has told him. What he hears takes precedence over his personal experience of Blanche and his initially favorable response. Disturbed that Blanche would deliberately present only one side of her character while duplicitously concealing the other, Mitch wants her to be only what others say she is. As scene 9 ends, he tries to force himself on her physically, demanding "what [he has] been missing all summer." His actions foreshadow Stanley's rape of Blanche that same night.

Another of Mitch's violent actions that likewise prepares the audience for what Stanley will later do makes it clear that the distance separating Mitch from Stanley is not all that great. Just before Blanche is led off to the sanatorium, Stanley tears the paper lantern from the light bulb. When Mitch enters two scenes earlier, armed with his incriminating proof, he demands to see Blanche in the bright glare of the naked bulb. He seems to think the light will not only reveal her true age and the effects of time upon her beauty—which it indeed will—but also provide evidence of her moral stature—which it cannot. For the harsh light, like the gossip, can reveal only the outer and not the inner, the material fact and not the spiritual truth that is susceptible only to Blanche's "magic." "*Tear[ing] the paper lantern off the light bulb*" (144) symbolically does violence to Blanche's person and integrity as much as the literal physical acts that Mitch will attempt and Stanley will accomplish. Little wonder that Mitch recognizes his complicity in

Blanche's destruction and mourns not only the lost possibility for himself but Blanche's departure into the world of the lost from which he potentially could have saved her. And her destruction, the death of the possibility for love if not of desire, will be Mitch's as well.

The Final Callers

The appearance of the heavy Matron *"in her severe dress"* and Blanche's terrified response imagistically recall the old woman peddling flowers for the dead two scenes earlier. The nurse, *"accompanied by . . . lurid reflections and noises of the jungle"* and *"divested of all the softer properties of womanhood"* (174–75) that Blanche so values and represents, is prematurely ready to straitjacket her patient. She becomes *"a peculiarly sinister figure,"* providing a foretaste of what awaits Blanche in the asylum. Her voice echoes and reverberates, expressionistically recalling the inhuman horror of the rape. Through another sound effect, Williams underscores the threatening nature of even the kindly Doctor. The Varsouviana, forever associated in Blanche's mind with the betrayal of love and the death of a loved one, is his music too; it plays both as he enters and when Blanche first sets eyes upon him.

The Doctor's gentle manner, once he is shorn of the *"cynical detachment [of] the state institution"* (171), temporarily calms Blanche's inner voices and anxieties as she accepts the small grace of "kindness" proffered by this "stranger." This is not the first time that Blanche has "depended on" either strangers or kindness, yet the earlier instances were usually fleeting. Blanche's "intimacies with strangers," for example, brought surcease from guilt and satisfied desire. And, at the end of scene 3, when Mitch attempts to relieve Blanche of her uneasiness over the volatile marriage of Stanley and Stella, she appreciates his "being so kind! I need kindness now" (69). His sheltering kindness, however, is only conditionally given and is soon replaced by cruelty. Likewise, the kindness of this Doctor of mercy may well be short–lived, to be replaced by the detached treatment of others less willing to sustain Blanche in her already precarious state of illusion.

The "magic" that Blanche has always tried to give to others, the lifting through art of their ordinary lives from the pedestrian to the ennobling, may fail her when she herself is most in need of it: she is still present enough in the world of reality to see that this Doctor is *not* Shep Huntleigh, the gentleman caller of her dreams. If Blanche was able, for a brief interval at the beginning of scene 10, to slip into the saving realm of fantasy after Mitch shattered any remaining hope for happiness in the world of reality, Stanley's attack has violated not only her body but her soul as well; he appears to have irreparably wounded her powers of imagination, of art—and the restoration of these has been at best partial by play's end. And the guilty Mitch sits helplessly and shamefully by.

A Streetcar Named Desire, scene 11; Blanche exits dependent on "the kindness of strangers."
Reproduced by permission of the Harry Ransom Humanities Research Center Library, University of Texas at Austin.

10

Further Perspectives

The preceding chapters on the style, structure, and characters of *A Streetcar Named Desire* have employed some of the most common critical approaches available to readers of literary works. These have included: the formalist approach that examines how Williams structures his play around a series of dichotomies (spirit/matter, gentility/brutality, harmless illusion/harmful delusion); the generic approach that considers whether *Streetcar* is a tragedy; the psychological approach that sees Blanche in light of studies about hysteria and Stanley from the perspective of the macho, dominating personality; the sociocultural approach that explores how the myth of Southern chivalry curtails Blanche's independence, as well as how utilitarian technology threatens the artistic sensibility; and the mythic perspective that finds in the decline of the South a new Fall from grace. Two other methods work in a sustained way: a literary-historical approach might position *Streetcar* in the context of the medieval "summoning by death" plays, while a feminist approach would focus on how society, through cultural conditioning, stereotypes gender roles, viewing them as character determinants.

"Streetcar" as a Dance of Death

Dramatists often draw upon well-established forms from earlier periods, openly exploiting their audience's knowledge to modulate their response. In this, Williams is no different; in both *Streetcar* and the preceding *Summer and Smoke* he employs the pattern of the medieval morality play. The full-scale morality dramas, such as *The Castle of Perseverance* (ca. 1425), follow humankind from birth to death, dramatizing the conflict of the Virtues and Vices as they struggle for the soul of a universalized, everyman figure. The most enduring and widely known of the medieval morality dramas, *Everyman* (ca. 1495), narrows its focus from human spiritual progress through all of life to center on the moment when Death comes to call Everyman to the grave. Death, iconographically clothed as a skeleton, is a dominant presence in *Everyman;* imagery of death also pervades *Streetcar.*

Williams's drama might well be seen as a modern variation on the medieval morality play: after a long struggle between opposing forces for her soul, the heroine is ushered off the stage, out of life. The work's title introduces the tension between "desire" and the as yet unnamed death—what Blanche will call its "opposite." Blanche's opening line contains the first specific reference to death in the name of the streetcar called "Cemeteries" she has just disembarked from. And even mingled with the celebratory occasion of birth in the play's closing scenes are images of death and burial at sea (something that Williams, in imitation of his poet hero Hart Crane, who provides the epigraph to *Streetcar,* himself longed for but was denied). The death imagery in *Streetcar* is so pervasive that the play becomes a veritable memento mori.

Twice, Blanche emphatically alludes to the allegorized icon of death come for humankind that is familiar from the moralities. In scene 1, she describes the Grim Reaper who had set up his "headquarters" on the steps of Belle Reve while Stella was "in bed with [her]—Polack!" (22) (Here, again, is the dichotomy between Eros and Thanatos.) Just as death followed the biblical Fall, all that remains of the new Eden of the DuBois family is a graveyard. In scene 9, Blanche personifies death once more when she tells Mitch that during her bedside watch over the last family member of the previous generation, "death was as close as you are" (149). If the link between "death" and "you"—that is, Mitch—in that line is unsettling, well it should be, since a few moments later he effectively removes whatever small hope still remains in Blanche for a normal, loving life.

Blanche's exposition in scenes 1, 6, and 9 of her former life in Laurel is also death-obsessed. She recounts to Stella "the long parade to the graveyard" (21) as one by one the remaining members of their family died horrible deaths. They then were buried in costly "gorgeous boxes" that belie the ugly suffering that came before interment on their reduced acreage. The high school principal who fires Blanche for her indiscretions, starting her on her final journey away from Belle Reve to the ironically named Elysian Fields, is Mr. Graves; the soldiers she uses sexually to assuage her guilt over having helped cause Allan's death, as well as to reaffirm life through desire, are gathered up "like daisies" (149) cut and wilting away in the paddy wagon to be taken back to camp. The deaths that define Mitch's past and present—his loss of the girl who vowed to "love [him] better after death" (57) and of the mother who will exert control over him beyond her life— parallel the way in which Blanche's existence is also bounded by the dying.

Finally, the two festive ritual occasions in *Streetcar* —the baby's literal birthday and Blanche's abortive birthday party—each carry overtones of death. Stella's child cannot help but remind Blanche of the motherhood that has been denied to her. The baby is the result of desire, perhaps even proof of love; yet Stanley, through his rape of Blanche, an act of animal passion devoid of humanizing affection, celebrates the birth of his son by betraying the sacredness of married sexuality and its regenerative potential. The birthday dinner for Blanche, interrupted by Stanley's violent outburst and left incomplete, the cake unserved, by Mitch's failure to arrive, is a precursor of her eventual death. Blanche is sensitive about her age because each passing year further subjects her physical beauty to the ravages of time. For the unmarried and childless Blanche, a birthday becomes a potent reminder of mortality, of the way that death overtakes desire—and love.

As Mitch moves closer to openly rejecting any possibility for marrying Blanche because of her sordid past, they are interrupted by another emblem of death, the blind old Mexican Woman "*in a dark shawl . . . faintly visible outside the building*" peddling "*Flores para los muertos*" (147), the bunches of brightly painted tin blossoms used in funeral processions and as gravesite decorations. Her sudden appearance disturbs and frightens Blanche, not just because these bouquets recall the "pretty flowers" associated with death at Belle Reve, but because she intuits that even more than Mitch's earlier roses promising eternal love, these flowers have an appropriateness for her. Significantly, the Mexican Woman's "soft mournful cries" continue in the background as Mitch's rejection metaphorically rings Blanche's death knell. In scene 11, as Blanche completes preparations to leave on her trip, the cathedral bells chime in the background. For Blanche, these bells, which contrast with the sounds of the blue piano throughout the play, are "the only clean thing in the Quarter" (170). If their ringing contributes to the religious aura of salvation that surrounds Blanche's leavetaking, they also toll for her, in the Donnean sense of marking death. And eerily present in summoning Blanche to a death-in-life at the asylum is the severely dressed Matron, Williams's modern analogue for the medieval figure of Death.

"Streetcar" as a Feminist Text

From his earliest plays, Williams possesses a deep understanding of feminine psychology and a special sympathy for his heroines: he admits to finding much of himself in Blanche and, conversely, of Blanche in himself. He can be viewed as an androgynous artist in whom the masculine and feminine sensibilities are almost perfectly poised—or some would claim tipped in favor of the feminine. This view opens him to accusations of sexual stereotyping in his characters, of presenting women as *naturally* more sensitive, feeling, and humane than their male counterparts. In her recent feminist study somewhat unfortunately and misleadingly entitled *Intercourse,* Andrea Dworkin, for example, distinguishes between the two protagonists of *A Streetcar Named Desire:* she sees Stanley as dehumanized since he is without an "interior life" and devoid of any awareness of the "consequence" of his acts, whereas Blanche is made "human" precisely because of her "capacity to suffer over sex" and "her opposition to ordinary masculinity" that results in her being "stigmatized."[34]

Raman Selden, in his handy introductory volume *Contemporary Literary Theory,* has formulated a list of foci around which one can center a discussion of sexual differences in a literary work and which can thus serve as a heuristic for examining a text from a feminist perspective. Selden's five points of departure involve issues of "biology," of "experience," of "discourse," of "the unconscious," and of "social and economic conditions."[35] Certainly *Streetcar* proves more amenable than virtually any other classic American drama to such an approach. If a male is to confirm the biological superiority that is stereotypically attributed to him, he needs a weaker inferior whom he can dominate and manipulate; male power, therefore, ordinarily requires assertion through physical means. In *Streetcar,* men view the women as existing by and large to be used for their own gratification and self-affirmation. The initial audience response sanctions Stanley's assertion of his authority through physical strength and control; Stella, in her wifely submissiveness, willingly consents to being a womb to be impregnated. As society idealizes and sanctifies the virginal woman for man's use in marriage, it also stigmatizes Blanche's experience of her own body as immoral; the double standard of repressive puritanism denies "desire" as appropriate for Blanche, thus increasing her guilt and driving her further toward neurosis. As a woman, Blanche faces social pressure to be sexual for the sake of the man, and yet society sanctions no other outlet for this sexuality than marriage, which might only be continued suppression, if of a different kind. For Stanley, Blanche's character is defined ultimately by the rape that he perpetrates, which he sees as neither more nor less than the logical and proper continuation of his victim's string of one-night stands.

In the world of *Streetcar,* the woman is faced with the need to assert her power by some means other than physical control, since in that arena she is (blessedly, Williams indicates) not man's equal, nor should she desire to be. The route of superiority open to her—and largely denied to or at least unrecognized by most men—is the avenue of the heart and the soul: affective and spiritual values like empathy, kindness, and grace. Her words and her gestures are intuitive and circuitous, as opposed to men's which are overly rational and pointedly linear. Blanche's poetic vocabulary, both of word and action, threatens the entrenched discourse of patriarchy. Her source of strength, her art, which depends upon softness and beauty and gentility, challenges the established discourse of power with its words like "stud" that bring down the curtain. But since her inner qualities are not widely valued in a pragmatic and materialistic society, they are rejected. Related to the discourse of patriarchy is the dominant economic system of capitalism that engenders a certain behavior. When they are young, women like Stella and Blanche are treated as ornaments rather than trained for economic independence. And though the women left behind during the war years entered occupations normally held by men, their activities threatened the balance of power once the soldiers returned home. So women were once again marginalized, returned to more seemly jobs in the home or on the fringes of productivity.

The ultimate marginalization of woman, as seen in Blanche, is the madness that Dworkin would argue is "a consequence of her sexual knowledge" (44). Denied any societally sanctioned experience of desire, Blanche becomes, by male standards, irrational, neurotic, and hysterical. She is finally institutionalized by a science—psychiatry—that is itself patriarchal in its definition of woman as lacking that which is man's by nature. Having faced the enforced death of desire at the hands of her "executioner," Blanche's only saving grace is to embrace death in the form of a madness that can effectively blank out the disparity between her condition of absolute physical powerlessness and the imaginative dreams that earlier sustained her.

11

The Themes

Unless they are by nature predisposed to be essayists or propagandists, dramatists do not write messages. Instead, they create characters who involve and move an audience through word and deed because, as the contemporary American playwright David Mamet says, they "bring to the stage the life of the soul."[36] If a drama retains its fascination and currency for audiences year after year, as *A Streetcar Named Desire* has done on the stage, the screen, and the page, it does so at first not by *what* it says but rather by the emotional experience it conveys through conflict, character, dialogue, setting, and symbol. The themes of a play emerge only upon reflection *after* the initial experience with the text as performed in the theater or acted out imaginatively in the mind. Nevertheless, when spectators or readers encounter a verbal rather than a purely visual or aural work of art, they are likely to ask: But what is the artist saying? What does it all mean? When such questions are raised about a play as rich and masterful as Williams's, it is easy enough to provide at least the beginnings of some answers.

"There's God—so quickly!"

As an epigraph to *Streetcar*, Williams chooses four lines from Hart Crane's poem, "The Broken Tower": "And so it was that I entered the broken world / To trace the visionary company of love, its voice / An instant in the wind (I know not whither hurled) / But not for long to hold each desperate choice." The import and appropriateness of these lines is apparent. Blanche finds herself in "a broken world" because the passage of time and social change means that the present cannot recapture the past. Her rejection of Allan has also caused her spiritual desolation, sexual longing, and psychological dislocation. "The visionary company of love"—potentially offered by Stella and then by Mitch—is the hoped for and nearly achieved salvation. Yet these moments of affirmation prove fleeting. Perhaps the key word in the epigraph is "visionary": Blanche's idealistic expectations place an almost transcendent faith in others that they are ill-prepared to live up to.

Streetcar is partially about the need for mutuality among human beings, about acting as God to others through responding to cries for help, especially of the desperate, the lonely, and the misfits of the world. To escape the usual human condition of self-centeredness and solipsism (Williams has said "Hell is yourself" [*Time*, 53]) and break through the barriers that separate demands not only pity, without any hint of condescension, for the physical, psychological and spiritual lot of others but compassion *without judgment*. If the universe sometimes seems silent and unresponsive to Williams's characters and their misery, they counter with their outgoing responsiveness to others.

This demands, however, a flexibility in ethical standards, a realization that one's own moral system might not be that of another. Yet if these frailties and weaknesses are understandably human and not hurtful to others, then they deserve to be treated compassionately. This demands that one's moral categories, especially in the realm of human sexuality, be flexible. In Williams's plays this requires understanding Allan's homosexuality in *Streetcar* or the salesman's underwear fetish in *The Night of the Iguana,* or simply accepting the near religious dimension of healthy physicality as a means of transcendence in *The Rose Tattoo.* To respond to another's needs—or to have one's needs met by the other—in unselfish yet simultaneously self-fulfilling love is perhaps the most that any of Williams's misbegotten creatures can hope to achieve.

"The . . . unforgivable sin"

Williams's wide-ranging call to respond to others in time of need is not a situation ethic that sanctions any and all actions. If sexuality when it is entered into lovingly can be a kind of salvation, it is also open to distortion or even perversion if it becomes merely a way to use or abuse another person for power, control or revenge. Stanley's rape of Blanche, for example, is willfully brutal and destructive. Whereas Stanley seems not to have a guilty bone in his body, others who act much less reprehensibly experience the guilt requisite to forgiveness. Such is the case with Blanche after her unthinking condemnation of Allan for his homosexuality.

If anything, Blanche is too unforgiving of her past and insists on punishing herself too harshly. Feeling too much guilt is as imbalanced in Williams's world as feeling too little; both are debilitating extremes. To become obsessed with the evil in oneself (and others), at the expense of recognizing the good, leads to inactivity and despair, to being so locked in the past that the present and future become circumscribed. The "sinner" is so closed in and consumed with guilt that he or she feels unworthy of being reached—and so becomes unreachable. Williams's world is a fallen world; navigating it humanly and humanely requires acceptance of that condition. We are flawed, but not so flawed that we should despair. The courage in the face of sinfulness that *The Night of the Iguana* counsels is what Blanche found lacking in herself in her confrontation with Allan, and is now in need of in her relationship with Mitch.

"A bargaining with mist and mold"

Williams frequently uses opposites or antinomies, such as flesh versus spirit, to suggest how a dichotomous rather than an integrative view of (wo)man serves only to fracture and fragment, severing one side of experience as if it were expendable. In *Streetcar,* succumbing to the demands of the flesh in an exploitative or totally selfish way can be destructive, but attempting to ignore the body will also result in imbalance, often leading to neuroticism. Desire cannot exist apart from the body; the call of the flesh must be responded to wisely and in a loving manner before it can be transcended—and then it neither can nor should be left totally behind.

The verses that the dying Nonno in *The Night of the Iguana* regards as his crowning poetic achievement are again instructive. On the natural plane, his final poem is about the cycle of birth, growth, harvest, and decay; the orange tree's fruit passes from ripeness and begins the process of returning to the earth from which it sprang. On the mythic level, the poem recounts a fall from a perfect world to an imperfect one—what the poet Gerard Manley Hopkins in "Spring and Fall" calls "goldengrove unleaving." On a more personal level, the poem reflects the need to move from the ideal to the real, from innocence to experience, without succumbing to a debilitating disillusionment. "The bargaining with mist and mold," "the plummeting to earth" in "an intercourse with earth's obscene corrupting love" (371) must be faced with gallantry, even though this is a more deeply frightening process for the human persona than for the living things in nature. To be fully human requires admission and acceptance of fallibility, sinfulness, corruptibility, and sexuality. The courage to accept this darker side without falling into despair is demonstrated, first, in the compassion given and received from the other; second, in a recognition of shared guilt; and, finally, through the aesthetic experience, particularly as creative artist but also as audience.

"The hand mirror . . . cracks"

If the saving grace of mutuality, then, is one of Williams's commanding themes, so is the awful truth of mutability; if an obsession with one's own guilt can destroy, so likewise can an overemphasis on time as loss create fear and anxiety. Time as the villain that corrupts and destroys is a given in Williams's world, particularly for his women, like Blanche or Alexandra del Lago in *Sweet Birth of Youth* (1959). They depend upon physical beauty and appeal to rescue them from aloneness through sex or, if they are lucky, love. Since Alexandra is an actress, she fears that a decline in artistic power (which also beset Williams in his later years) is inevitably linked with waning physical beauty: what is the "out-crying heart of an artist"[37]—who feels impelled to continue in her vocation—to do in the face of a hostile audience and critics (something, again, the playwright also faced)? Blanche's art and creation might seem at first glance mainly internal and private, the remembering and partial reinventing of a past that perhaps never was at Belle Reve, and assuredly never was in Shep Huntleigh. Yet her art is likewise external and public: she assumes masks or roles with others, supported by her costumes and makeup.

Time and age ravage and destroy the physical, so that finally even the mirror that for so long sent back a reflection of youth can no longer lie, but speaks of encroaching mortality. When Blanche gazes into the mirror, she sees an image that she has not herself reproduced through a child. As Blanche looks into the mirror and slams it down so that the glass cracks, she appears to suffer a breaking of the spirit just before Stanley breaks her body. In a world peopled and controlled by Stanleys, appearances are all; only phenomena that can be measured count. Not subject, however, to time's diminishment but, instead, potentially brought to fruition in the fullness of time are those inner, spiritual beauties that Blanche, despite her outer physical, economic, and emotional destitution, can claim for herself. Such spiritual beauties, so easily misunderstood and undervalued, are mainly amenable to expression in art. As Williams writes in "The Timeless World of a Play," his introduction to *The Rose Tattoo*, "the continual rush of time, so violent that it appears to be screaming . . . deprives our actual lives of so much dignity and meaning, and it is, perhaps more than anything else, the *arrest of time* which has taken place in a completed work of art that gives to certain plays their feeling of depth and significance" (*Essays*, 49).

"I want magic!"

If, in the face of life's impermanence and flux, the only thing guaranteed to endure is art, then it becomes understandable why Blanche has escaped into its world so incessantly. If she could freeze herself in the midst of an illusion (and the text is ambiguous whether or not she can), then she could stop her self-imposed punishment by ceasing to remember the truth of the past and finding peace in the sanitorium—as Williams's own beloved sister Rose was able to do. But art, for Williams as for Blanche, possesses a moral dimension beyond the merely escapist possibilities, revealing what humankind might and should become. Furthermore, art is of almost infinite worth to civilization's progress: *Streetcar,* like Chekhov's plays, valorizes beauty over use, spiritual worth over utilitarian price, Blanche's "wayward flashes" of "revelation" (*Essays,* 57) over Stanley's total dependence upon "empiric evidence." Williams joins Blanche in her fear that the Stanleys are taking over the world, knowing that without her and those like her the world would be emotionally and ethically poorer, and that an irreversible downward spiral would begin. It is a premonition of entropy, of disorder and return to primal chaos. *Streetcar*'s final message, its almost apocalyptic warning, is underscored by the roar of the locomotive that is blind, mechanistic progress on the move.

The antidote, for the audience as well as for Blanche, is art, which becomes for Williams a kind of secular sacrament. The audience at *Streetcar* enters the theater only to see one of the characters, Blanche, transform the stage into a theater of her own which she attempts to control by decorating the stage, directing the script, and playing the major role. Blanche's actions as artist keep before the audience the presence of Williams the artist as well; and her credo of truth through illusion and of the moral imperative of art to raise humankind beyond what it is by showing "what *ought* to be true" is Williams's credo, too. When the artistic act remains interior and thus private—merely an illusion or delusion in the mind—it requires only the self to do the imagining, which is possibly a close analogy to a retreat into madness. Williams intimates strongly, though, that art should not be exclusively an interior act but must reach out to others. When art is staged or made public, it demands the consent of the spectators/readers to the "make-believe." This act of faith from a community (that, in turn, is potentially enlightened and renewed) sanctions and sanctifies the illusion. But in *Streetcar*, unfortunately, the other characters, the onstage audience to Blanche, withhold that assent from her truth. Blanche leaves the theater stage Williams has created to enter another house of illusions, desirous of finding a destination at play's end that can assuage her loneliness and guilt. If the illusion is not permanent (and the play does not guarantee that, for Blanche, it will be), then the pain can return. The peculiar travail of the artist—both the Blanches and Williamses of this world—is that the "magic" of the art work is never sufficient unto itself and must be renewed through continued creative activity.

A half-dozen years before Tennessee Williams's death, Walter Kerr, whom many consider the "dean" of American theater critics in the period since World War II, wrote that "Williams's voice is the most distinctively poetic, the most idiosyncratically moving, and at the same time the most firmly dramatic to have come the American theater's way—ever. . . . He is our best playwright, and let qualifications go hang."[38] While the intense feeling and lyricism of Williams's works do not alone denote him as peculiarly American, perhaps two of his recurrent motifs, both abundantly evident in *Streetcar*, do: first, the disparity between dream and reality, between the long sought for Eden and the fallen paradise we inhabit; and, second, the disjunction (pervasive, too, in the works of America's first major dramatist, Eugene O'Neill) between the poet and the materialist—the determined factualist, getter and keeper of things who sees beauty as expendable or, worse still, a threat. As Williams himself remarks, *Streetcar* is finally about this "ravishment of the tender, the sensitive, the delicate, by the savage and brutal forces of modern society."[39] Standing as challenges against such brutalization are the best of Williams's plays, *The Glass Menagerie, Streetcar, Cat on a Hot Tin Roof, The Night of the Iguana.* And by common consent, the greatest of these is *A Streetcar Named Desire*, which the dramatist judged his "best play" (*Conversations*, 52).

Notes

1. Chester E. Eisinger, ed., *The 1940's: Profile of a Nation in Crisis* (Garden City, N.Y.: Doubleday Anchor, 1969), xiv–xviii.

2. "The Angel of the Odd," *Time*, 9 March 1962, 53.

3. Arthur Miller, *Timebends: A Life* (New York: Grove Press, 1987), 182.

4. Martin Gottfried, *A Theater Divided: The Postwar American Stage* (Boston: Little, Brown, 1967), 250; Jordan Y. Miller, ed., *Twentieth Century Interpretations of "A Streetcar Named Desire"* (Englewood Cliffs, N. J.: Prentice-Hall, 1971), 9.

5. Joseph Wood Krutch, "Review of *Streetcar Named Desire*," and Irwin Shaw, "Masterpiece," both in Miller, *Interpretations*, 40; 45.

6. Brooks Atkinson, "*Streetcar* Tragedy—Mr. Williams' Report on Life in New Orleans," and John Mason Brown, "Southern Discomfort," both in Miller, *Interpretations*, 32; 43.

7. Ward Morehouse, "New Hit Named *Desire*," Robert Coleman, "*Desire Streetcar* in for Long Run," and Louis Kronenberger, "A Sharp Southern Drama by Tennessee Williams," all in *New York Theatre Critics' Reviews* 8 (1947), 250–51.

8. Tennessee Williams, *Where I Live: Selected Essays*, ed. Christine R. Day and Bob Woods (New York: New Directions, 1978), 93. Hereafter cited by *Essays* and page number within the text.

9. George Jean Nathan, "The Streetcar Isn't Drawn by Pegasus," in Miller, *Interpretations*, 37; and Mary McCarthy, *Theatre Chronicles 1937–1962* (New York: Farrar, Straus, 1963), 131–35.

10. Elia Kazan, "Notebook for *A Streetcar Named Desire*," in *Directors on Directing: A Sourcebook of the Modern Theatre*, ed. Toby Cole and Helen Krich Chinoy (Indianapolis: Bobbs Merrill, 1976), 364–66. Hereafter cited by "Notebook" and page number within the text.

11. Eric Bentley, "Better than Europe?" in *In Search of Theater* (New York: Knopf, 1953), 87.

12. Jessica Tandy, "Letter 2 November 1948," in *Tennessee Williams, Dictionary of Literary Biography Documentary Series,* vol. 4, ed. Margaret A. VanAntwerp and Sally Jones (Detroit: Gale Research, 1984), 105. Hereafter cited by Letter and page number within the text.

13. Harold Clurman, "Tennessee Williams," in *The Divine Pastime: Theatre Essays* (New York: Macmillan, 1974), 11–12; 13–14.

14. Miller, *Interpretations,* 11–12.

15. Kathleen Hulley, "The Fate of the Symbolic in *A Streetcar Named Desire,*" in *Themes in Drama 4 (Drama and Symbolism),* ed. James Redmond (Cambridge: Cambridge University Press, 1982), 96.

16. Anea Vlasopolos, "Authorizing History: Victimization in *A Streetcar Named Desire,*" *Theatre Journal* 38 (October 1986): 325, 326, 328, 332.

17. Thomas E. Porter, *Myth and Modern American Drama* (Detroit: Wayne State University Press, 1969), 176.

18. Robert Brustein, "Designs for Living(Rooms)," review of Frank Rich and Lisa Aronson's *The Theatre Art of Boris Aronson, New Republic,* 1 February 1988, 29.

19. Tennessee Williams, *The Glass Menagerie* (New York: New Directions, 1966), 22. Hereafter cited by page number within the text.

20. Virginia Woolf, "Mr. Bennett and Mrs. Brown," in *The Captain's Deathbed and Other Essays* (New York: Harcourt Brace, 1950), 94, 97, 103.

21. C. W. E. Bigsby, *Joe Orton* (London: Methuen, 1982), 16.

22. Albert J. Devlin, ed., *Conversations with Tennessee Williams* (Jackson: University Press of Mississippi, 1986), 65. Hereafter cited by *Conversations* and page number within the text.

23. Paul Chodoff, "The Diagnosis of Hysteria: An Overview," *American Journal of Psychiatry* 131 (October 1974): 1073–78; and "Hysteria and Women," *American Journal of Psychiatry* 139 (May 1982): 545–51.

24. Tennessee Williams, *The Night of the Iguana,* in *The Theatre of Tennessee Williams,* vol. 4 (New York: New Directions, 1972), 363–64. Hereafter cited by page number within the text.

25. Arthur Miller, "Tragedy and the Common Man," in *The Theater Essays of Arthur Miller,* ed. Robert A. Martin (New York: Penguin, 1978), 4.

26. *New York Theatre Critics' Reviews* 8 (1947): 249–52.

27. Robert Emmet Jones, "Tennessee Williams's Early Heroines," in *Two Modern American Tragedies,* ed. John D. Hurrell (New York: Charles Scribner's Sons, 1961), 116.

28. Harry Taylor, "The Dilemma of Tennessee Williams," in Hurrell, *Tragedies,* 99.

Notes

29. Alfred Kazin, "Portrait of a Lady," review of R. W. B. Lewis and Nancy Lewis, eds., *The Letters of Edith Wharton, New Republic,* 29 August 1988, 42.

30. Quoted in Jennifer Allen, "The Man on the High Horse," *Esquire,* November 1988, 146.

31. Arno Gruen, *The Betrayal of the Self: The Fear of Autonomy in Men and Women,* trans. Hildegarde and Hunter Hannum (New York: Grove, 1988), 1–2; 31–32; 59; 64; 73; 77.

32. Bentley, *Search,* 88.

33. Henry I. Schvey, "Madonna at the Poker Night: Pictorial Elements in Tennessee Williams' *A Streetcar Named Desire,*" in *From Cooper to Philip Roth: Essays on American Literature,* ed. J. Bakker and D. R. M. Wilkinson (Amsterdam: Rodopi, 1980), 72.

34. Andrea Dworkin, *Intercourse* (New York: The Free Press, 1987), 41–42.

35. Raman Selden, *A Reader's Guide to Contemporary Literary Theory* (Lexington: University Press of Kentucky, 1985), 130.

36. David Mamet, *Writing in Restaurants* (New York: Penguin, 1986), viii.

37. Tennessee Williams, *Sweet Bird of Youth* (New York: New Directions, 1972), 35.

38. Walter Kerr, "A Touch of the Poet Isn't Enough to Sustain Williams's Latest Play," *New York Times,* 22 May 1977, D5.

39. Quoted in Charles Higham, *Brando: The Unauthorized Biography* (New York: New American Library, 1987), 58.

Bibliography

Primary Works

Standard Edition of Tennessee Williams's Works

New Directions, the dramatist's longtime publisher, has reprinted his plays in a collected edition of seven volumes, *The Theatre of Tennessee Williams,* published between 1971 and 1981.

Plays

Camino Real. Norfolk, Conn.: New Directions, 1953.

Cat on a Hot Tin Roof. New York: New Directions, 1955.

Clothes for a Summer Hotel. New York: New Directions, 1983.

Dragon Country: A Book of Plays. New York: New Directions, 1969.

The Eccentricities of a Nightingale. New York: Dramatists Play Service, 1977.

The Glass Menagerie. New York: New Directions, 1945.

The Gnädiges Fräulein. New York: Dramatists Play Service, 1967.

In the Bar of a Tokyo Hotel. New York: Dramatists Play Service, 1969.

Kingdom of Earth (The Seven Descents of Myrtle). New York: New Directions, 1968.

A Lovely Sunday for Creve Coeur. New York: New Directions, 1980.

The Milk Train Doesn't Stop Here Anymore. New York: New Directions, 1964.

The Mutilated. New York: The Dramatists Play Service, 1967.

The Night of the Iguana. New York: New Directions, 1962.

Orpheus Descending, with Battle of Angels. New York: New Directions, 1958.

Out Cry. New York: New Directions, 1970.

Bibliography

Period of Adjustment. New York: New Directions, 1960.
The Red Devil Battery Sign. New York: New Directions, 1988.
The Rose Tattoo. New York: New Directions, 1951.
Small Craft Warnings. New York: New Directions, 1972.
A Streetcar Named Desire. New York: New Directions, 1947.
Suddenly Last Summer. New York: New Directions, 1948.
Summer and Smoke. New York: New Directions, 1948.
Sweet Bird of Youth. New York: New Directions, 1959.
27 Wagons Full of Cotton and Other One-Act Plays. Norfolk, Conn.: New Directions, 1945.
Vieux Carré. New York: New Directions, 1979.
You Touched Me! (with Donald Windham). New York: Samuel French, 1947.

Screenplays

Baby Doll. New York: New Directions, 1956.
Stopped Rocking and Other Screenplays. New York: New Directions, 1984.

Fiction

Eight Mortal Ladies Possessed: A Book of Stories. New York: New Directions, 1974.
Hard Candy: A Book of Stories. New York: New Directions, 1954.
Knightly Quest: A Novella and Four Short Stories. New York: New Directions, 1966.
Moise and the World of Reason. New York: Simon and Schuster, 1975.
One Arm and Other Stories. New York: New Directions, 1948.
The Roman Spring of Mrs. Stone. New York: New Directions, 1950.
Tennessee Williams: The Collected Stories. New York: New Directions, 1985.

Poetry

Androgyne, Mon Amour: Poems. New York: New Directions, 1977.
In the Winter of Cities. Norfolk, Conn.: New Directions, 1956.

Autobiography

Memoirs. Garden City, N.Y.: Doubleday, 1975.

Essays

Where I Live: Selected Essays. Edited by Christine R. Day and Bob Woods. New York: New Directions, 1978.

Letters

Tennessee Williams's Letters to Donald Windham 1940–65. Edited by Donald Windham. New York: Holt, Rinehart and Winston, 1977.

Interviews

Conversations with Tennessee Williams. Edited by Albert J. Devlin. Jackson: University Press of Mississippi, 1986.

Secondary Works

Biography

Rader, Dotson. *Tennessee: Cry of the Heart.* Garden City, N.Y.: Doubleday, 1985. A friend's gossipy and anecdotal personal reminiscence.

Spoto, Donald. *The Kindness of Strangers: The Life of Tennessee Williams.* Boston: Little, Brown, 1985. In the absence of an authorized critical biography, the most complete, if somewhat dull and dispassionate, look at the dramatist's colorful life.

Williams, Edwina Dakin (as told to Lucy Freeman). *Remember Me to Tom.* New York: G. P. Putnam's Sons, 1963. A mother's memoir about her famous son's life and career up through his psychoanalysis in the late fifties; reprints a selection of letters.

Critical Studies: Books

Bigsby, C. W. E. *A Critical Introduction to Twentieth-Century American Drama 2: Williams/Miller/Albee.* Cambridge: Cambridge University Press, 1984. A solid analysis of the playwright's canon, focusing on ambiguity, determinism, and the motif of art.

Fedder, Norman J. *The Influence of D. H. Lawrence on Tennessee Williams.* The Hague: Mouton, 1966. Discusses Williams as Lawrence's artistic heir in his emphasis on the importance of feeling and sensual values over rationalism and materialism.

Bibliography

Hurrell, John D., ed. *Two Modern American Tragedies: Reviews and Criticism of "Death of a Salesman" and "A Streetcar Named Desire".* New York: Charles Scribner's Sons, 1961. Collects reviews and other early brief treatments of *Streetcar*.

Jackson, Esther Merle. *The Broken World of Tennessee Williams.* Madison: University of Wisconsin Press, 1966. Focuses on Williams's poetic techniques and how they contribute to the development of a new form in his plays.

Jones, David Richard. *Great Directors at Work: Stanislavsky, Brecht, Kazan, Brook.* Berkeley: University of California Press, 1986. A masterful account of Kazan's original approach to translating *Streetcar* from script to stage.

Miller, Jordan Y., ed. *Twentieth Century Interpretations of "A Streetcar Named Desire": A Collection of Critical Essays.* Englewood Cliffs, N. J.: Prentice-Hall, 1971. Reprints reviews and essays, including important studies by Weissman, von Szeliski, and Riddell.

Nelson, Benjamin. *Tennessee Williams: The Man and His Work.* New York: Obolensky, 1961. A dependable reading of Williams's dramatic techniques and themes through the plays of the fifties.

Phillips, Gene D. *The Films of Tennessee Williams.* East Brunswick, N. J.: Associated University Presses, 1980. Examines the changes that were made in adapting Williams's plays to the screen.

Porter, Thomas E. *Myth and Modern American Drama.* Detroit: Wayne State University Press, 1969. Includes an enlightening chapter on the myth of the South in *Streetcar*.

Sievers, W. David. *Freud on Broadway: A History of Psychoanalysis and the American Drama.* New York: Hermitage House, 1955. The standard overview of the subject, proposing *Streetcar* as a quintessential example.

Stanton, Stephen S. *Tennessee Williams: A Collection of Critical Essays.* Englewood Cliffs, N. J.: Prentice-Hall, 1977. Reprints fifteen major articles from the mid-sixties through the mid-seventies.

Tharpe, Jac, ed. *Tennessee Williams: A Tribute.* Jackson: University Press of Mississippi, 1977. Contains seven original essays on *Streetcar*.

Thompson, Judith J. *Tennessee Williams's Plays: Memory, Myth, and Symbol* (University of Kansas Humanistic Studies 54). New York: Peter Lang, 1987. An existential and archetypal reading of the plays, including a thorough exploration of classical allusions and analogues.

Tischler, Nancy M. *Tennessee Williams: Rebellious Puritan.* New York: Citadel Press, 1961. Sees Williams as a romantic artist, drawing generously upon autobiography.

Critical Studies: Articles and Chapters of Books

Asselineau, Roger. "The Tragic Transcendentalism of Tennessee Williams," in *The Transcendentalist Constant in American Literature*, 153–62. New York: New York University Press, 1980. Discusses Williams's tendency to idealize sexual desire as a means of transcending the material.

Barranger, Milly S. "New Orleans as Theatrical Image in Plays by Tennessee Williams." *Southern Quarterly* 23 (Winter 1985): 38–54. Explores how the contrasts between Old World charm and urbanization in the playwright's favorite city contribute to the themes of several plays.

Berkman, Leonard. "The Tragic Downfall of Blanche DuBois." *Modern Drama* 10 (December 1967):249–57. Concludes that Blanche's tragedy resides in acceptance of a future with strangers that she had fought against.

Bock, Hedwig. "Tennessee Williams: Southern Playwright." In *Essays on Contemporary American Drama*, edited by Hedwig Bock and Albert Wertheim, 5–18. Munich: Max Hueber Verlag, 1981. Discusses the relationship between the southern myth and psychological neuroses, as well as the images and symbols Williams uses to explicate the subconscious.

Callahan, Edward F. "Tennessee Williams's Two Worlds." *North Dakota Quarterly* 25 (Summer 1957):61–67. Focuses on the Manichaean duality in the plays; sees Stella as a new Eve choosing between alternatives.

Cardullo, Bert. "The Blind Mexican Woman in Williams's *A Streetcar Named Desire*." *Notes on Modern American Literature* 7 (Fall 1983):item 14. Sees the flower seller as a symbol of death and Blanche's fate.

———. "The Role of The Baby in *A Streetcar Named Desire*." *Notes on Contemporary Literature* 14 (March 1984):4–5. Argues that the child ultimately comes between Stanley and Stella.

Clurman, Harold. "Tennessee Williams," in *The Divine Pastime: Theatre Essays*. New York: Macmillan, 1974, 11–18. The most comprehensive and substantive production review ever accorded *Streetcar*.

Corrigan, Mary Ann. "Realism and Theatricalism in *A Streetcar Named Desire*." *Modern Drama* 19 (December 1976):385–96. A seminal essay on expressionistic techniques and symbolic techniques that reveal what occurs in the characters' minds.

Hulley, Kathleen. "The Fate of the Symbolic in *A Streetcar Named Desire*." In *Themes in Drama 4 (Drama and Symbolism)*, edited by James Redmond, 89–99. Cambridge: Cambridge University Press, 1982. A semiotic approach that sees the play's characters as creating conflicting theatrical productions.

Kazan, Elia. "Notebook for *A Streetcar Named Desire*." In *Directors on Directing: A Source Book of the Modern Theatre*, edited by Toby Cole and Helen Krich Chinoy, 364–379. Indianapolis: Bobbs-Merrill, 1976.

Bibliography

An invaluable record of the original director's interpretation of *Streetcar* and its characters.

Mood, John J. "The Structure of *A Streetcar Named Desire.*" *Ball State University Forum* 14 (Summer 1973):9–10. Examines how Blanche's opening speech provides a clue to the play's design.

Quarino, Leonard. "The Cards Indicate a Voyage on *A Streetcar Named Desire.*" In *Tennessee Williams: 13 Essays,* edited by Jac Tharpe, 29–48. Jackson: University Press of Mississippi, 1980. Explores Williams's use of imagery from games of chance and luck; sees Blanche's journey as a metaphor for tragic voyage through life.

Schvey, Henry I. "Madonna at the Poker Night: Pictorial Elements in Tennessee Williams's *A Streetcar Named Desire.*" In *From Cooper to Philip Roth: Essays on American Literature,* edited by J. Bakker and D. R. M. Wilkinson, 70–77. Amsterdam: Rodopi, 1980. An insightful look at Williams's visual symbolism.

Taylor, Jo Beth. "*A Streetcar Named Desire:* Evolution of Blanche and Stanley." *Publications of the Mississippi Philological Association* (1986):63–66. Explores the genesis of Williams's characters in his earlier works.

Vlasopolos, Anea. "Authorizing History: Victimization in *A Streetcar Named Desire.*" *Theatre Journal* 38 (October 1986):322–38. A feminist reading that sees Stanley's discourse of patriarchy as challenging Blanche's interpretive authority.

Index

Index

About the Author

Thomas P. Adler holds A.B. and A.M. degrees from Boston College, and a Ph.D. from the University of Illinois at Urbana-Champaign. A teacher of medieval, Tudor, and modern dramatic literature, as well as of film history and aesthetics, he is professor of English at Purdue University in West Lafayette, Indiana. He has also served as associate dean of the Graduate School and is now associate dean of the School of Liberal Arts. The author of two previous studies of American theater—*Robert Anderson* (1978) and *Mirror on the Stage: The Pulitzer Plays as an Approach to American Drama* (1987)—he has written numerous book chapters and articles on such British and American playwrights as Shaw, O'Neill, Wilder, Inge, Wesker, Albee, Pinter, Rabe, Storey, Kopit, and Shepard. Included among his dozen previous essays and reviews on Williams are two reprinted in *Tennessee Williams: A Collection of Critical Essays* (1977) and, most recently, "When Ghosts Supplant Memories: *Clothes for a Summer Hotel*," which appeared in *The Southern Literary Journal,* and "Monologues and Mirrors in *Sweet Bird of Youth*" for *Critical Essays on Tennessee Williams.* Adler has also coauthored a rhetoric text, *The Writer's Choices* (2d ed., 1988).